A VICTORIAN AMERICAN
HENRY WADSWORTH LONGFELLOW

HENRY WADSWORTH LONGFELLOW
From a painting by C. P. A. Healey, 1862

DESIRES

RIGHT & WRONG

The Ethics of Enough

Mortimer J. Adler

Macmillan Publishing Company
New York

Maxwell Macmillan Canada
Toronto

Maxwell Macmillan International
New York • Oxford • Singapore • Sydney

Macmillan Publishing Company   Maxwell Macmillan Canada, Inc.
866 Third Avenue   1200 Eglinton Avenue East
New York, NY 10022   Suite 200
                                      Don Mills, Ontario M3C 3N1

Macmillan Publishing Company is part of the Maxwell Communication Group
of Companies.

Library of Congress Cataloging-in-Publication Data
Adler, Mortimer Jerome,———
   Desires, right & wrong: the ethics of enough/Mortimer J. Alder.
   p. cm.
   Includes index.
   ISBN 0-02-500281-3
   1. Ethics. 2. Desire (Philosophy) I. Title. II. Title: Desires, right and wrong.
   BJ1012.A29   1991   91-16382   CIP
   170—dc20

Designed by M 'N O Production Services, Inc.

Printed in the United States of America

CONTENTS

DESIRES
RIGHT & WRONG

PROLOGUE

Retrospective and Prospective

1

IT HAS BECOME CUSTOMARY for museums and galleries to stage retrospective exhibitions of the works of prominent painters. In some instances, the paintings are arranged according to successive periods of the painter's work.

The comparison may be somewhat farfetched, but this book is like a retrospective assemblage of a philosopher's successive efforts to deal with the major issues in ethics. Fifty years ago, in 1940, after conducting seminars at the University of Chicago during the preceding ten years, seminars in which treatises in moral philosophy were the subject of discussion, I wrote a book entitled *The Dialectic of Morals*. In it, I presented the sequence of questions and answers that occurred in college classes in which I tried to combat the then prevalent skepticism of students concerning ethics—their addiction to subjectivism and relativism about all questions of value, about the principles of morality, about the objective and universal truth of any statement that declared how human beings ought to conduct their lives in

1

order to live well. It is a current illusion that such skepticism on the part of students, not to mention their professors, first emerged in the late 1960s. On the contrary, it has been endemic in this century.

The Dialectic of Morals was published in 1941 and is now out of print. It contained, in seminal form, all the basic insights about real and apparent goods, about the mistake of thinking that pleasure is the only good, about virtue and happiness, that had clarified my own understanding of moral problems as a result of reading the dialogues of Plato and especially the *Nicomachean Ethics* of Aristotle. I should add that these insights also opened my eyes to the bankruptcy of moral philosophy in modern times, because of the serious errors made by David Hume, Immanuel Kant, John Stuart Mill, and John Dewey.

Thirty years later, in 1970, I wrote another book that is now out of print. It was entitled *The Time of Our Lives: The Ethics of Common Sense*. By this time, I had become persuaded that Aristotle's *Nicomachean Ethics* was the only eminently practical, philosophically sound, and thoroughly undogmatic treatise in moral philosophy that had been written in the twenty-five centuries of Western thought.

Of course, Aristotle's *Ethics* contained some errors (e.g., about natural slaves and the inferiority of women), but no human work is ever error free. Also, of course, the commentaries written by later Aristotelians sharpened some points, added significant elaborations, even contributed analytical refinements and new supporting arguments. But the advances that any of us who call ourselves Aristotelians can claim to have made are little more than embellishments on the body of Aristotelian thought.

For example, in *The Time of Our Lives*, my point of departure was to introduce the main features of Aristotle's

Ethics to twentieth-century readers in terms of the parts of human life that occupy the hours of our days—sleep, work, play, leisure, and rest—without ever mentioning Aristotle or using the fundamental concepts and principles of his moral philosophy. I followed that up by developing at much greater length and to much greater depth the basic insights that were to be found in *The Dialectic of Morals*, written thirty years earlier.

I also more fully expressed my critique of the inadequacies and mistakes of modern thinkers in the field of ethics, philosophers who either had not read Aristotle at all or had not read him carefully enough to understand him accurately and to perceive the substantial truth of his doctrine.

At that time, I was so impressed by the extraordinary misunderstandings to be found in the writings of modern philosophers, especially those in the nineteenth and twentieth centuries, who wrote commentaries on Aristotle's *Ethics*, that I appended a long Postscript to *The Time of Our Lives* in which I wrote my own thoroughly documented commentary on the *Ethics* in order to expose clearly the mistakes that had been made by others.

The Time of Our Lives has been out of print for many years. I am, therefore, republishing in Appendix II the Postscript to that book. I think readers will find it an enlightening commentary on Aristotle's *Ethics*. In Appendix I, I have put excerpts from the endnotes of *The Time of Our Lives*, especially passages that deal with the mistakes in moral philosophy made by Hume, Kant, Mill, and Dewey.

In the 1988 issue of *Great Ideas Today*, of which I am editor, I published an article that I had written, entitled "Ethics: Fourth Century B.C. and Twentieth Century A.D." That essay was a critique of two recent books in moral philosophy, one by Alasdair MacIntyre, *After Virtue* (1981), and one by Bernard Williams, *Ethics and the Limits of Philosophy* (1985). Both books were alike in their qualified praise of Aristotle's *Ethics* as the outstanding contribution of Greek antiquity to moral philosophy. But each qualified that commendation, MacIntyre by attempting to point out inadequacies and errors in Aristotle's thought that had to be, and could be, repaired in the twentieth century; and Williams by arguing that, although Aristotle's treatise was sound enough for Athenians in the fourth century B.C., it was no longer sound in the twentieth century, adding that philosophy in our century had nothing to take its place.[1]

After the foregoing digression concerning the mistakes of two contemporary philosophers who are distinguished by their qualified praise of the soundness of Aristotle's *Ethics*, I return to the strict chronology of my earlier writings in moral philosophy.

Since *The Time of Our Lives* in 1970, the books I have written on other subjects contained chapters that treat, in different contexts, the basic principles and concepts expressed in the abiding truth of Aristotle's moral philosophy.

Part III of *Aristotle for Everybody*, published in 1978, was entitled "Man the Doer." The chapter titles of Part III manifest the course of the argument: Thinking about Ends and Means; Living and Living Well; Good, Better, Best; How to Pursue Happiness; Good Habits and Good Luck;

---

1. In *The Great Ideas Today, 1982,* I had earlier published a more extensive critique of MacIntyre's *After Virtue,* an abbreviated version of which I wrote in my 1988 essay. The central point of both critiques was that nothing in twentieth-century thought, experience, society, or the conditions of human life had rendered Aristotle's *Ethics* any less sound today than it was in Greek antiquity; nor was there any need in this century to modify Aristotle's thought in essentials in order to make it intellectually respectable or more palatable to current prejudices. Both of these critical essays have been reprinted in my book *Reforming Education: The Closing of the American Mind,* published in 1989. That is still in print.

What Others Have a Right to Expect from Us; What We Have a Right to Expect from Others and from the State.

In *Six Great Ideas*, published in 1981, four chapters on the idea of goodness treated the distinction between "is" and "ought"; the distinction between real and apparent goods; the range and scale of goods; and the ultimate and common good.

In *A Vision of the Future*, published in 1984, a book that I regarded as dealing with six not so great ideas, there was a chapter on wealth, with a section on money, and a chapter on virtue and happiness. Though the latter recapitulated insights and truths that had been expressed earlier in *The Time of Our Lives* and in *Aristotle for Everybody*, these books were at that time out of print and I felt justified in repeating matters covered earlier, always, of course, with additions and elaborations necessitated by a difference in the context in which they occurred.

The same thing must be said of *Ten Philosophical Mistakes*, published in 1985, which dealt with errors that are characteristically and exclusively modern errors, since the sixteenth century. In this book there were, once more, somewhat repetitive chapters, one on moral values and one on happiness and contentment, but once again with difference in both emphasis and detail because the context called for identifying the mistakes about these matters that were typically and peculiarly modern.

In the light of this retrospective account of my earlier writings in the field of moral philosophy, some now out of print and some still available, readers would be justified in wondering whether this is still another repetition of the same materials, and in asking what is new and additionally instructive in this book.

My response is twofold. On the one hand, a certain

amount of repetition is unavoidable and, since in my judgment, the oft-repeated truths are of such great importance in contemporary life, even greater now than they were ten and twenty years ago, I proceed without apology in this respect. On the other hand, as the title of this book indicates, the approach is new and many of the problems here to be considered have not been treated in any of my earlier books, certainly not in the detail that they deserve.

2

It is fitting that the new approach should focus on desire, for it is that term which is the key to the treasure of practical wisdom in Aristotle's moral philosophy. The opening sentence of his *Ethics* calls our attention to the fact that "every action and pursuit is thought to aim at some good" and it is for this reason that "the good has rightly been declared to be that at which all things aim."

It is a simple step from this sentence to the axiomatic propositions that the good is the desirable and the desirable the good.

In the third book of the *Ethics*, we learn that in the sphere of human appetites, there are two radically distinct modes of desire. This throws light on the double meaning of the axiom about the good being the desirable and the desirable the good; for the word "desirable" can mean either that something is actually desired or that it ought to be desired. It may be actually desired when it ought not to be desired and it may be something that ought to be desired when it is not actually desired. This distinction between two modes of desire is an ethical distinction, not a psychological one.

In the sixth book of the *Ethics*, again in a single sentence,

Aristotle employs desire to solve the crucial problem of moral philosophy, particularly in the form in which that problem is stated in the twentieth century. The current prevalent skepticism about the objective validity of all value judgments and all statements containing the words "ought" or "ought not" derives from the puzzle that modern and contemporary philosophers have completely failed to solve.

If truth lies in the correspondence of our descriptive judgments about what is or is not with the way things are or are not, how can there be any truth in prescriptive judgments that state what ought or ought not to be done or sought? Aristotle's answer to that question declares that the truth of normative or prescriptive judgments, or of value judgments about what is good or evil, desirable or undesirable, consists in the conformity of such judgments to right desire.

That single sentence in Book VI of the *Ethics* was noted, of course, by such disciples of Aristotle as Thomas Aquinas in the thirteenth century; but it has been completely overlooked by modern philosophers, especially by those who have declared ethics to be a noncognitive discipline because it lies outside the sphere of disciplines in which there is testable truth and falsity.

The problem that Aristotle disposed of in a single sentence requires a great deal more to be said in order to make that single sentence fully intelligible and to develop all of its implications; but this is not the place to do that. For our present purposes, let it suffice to show the centrality and importance of desire as the pivotal term in Aristotle's moral philosophy.

There are still further indications of this fact. That moral virtue is a pivotal term in Aristotle's *Ethics* is generally acknowledged, even by those who do not recognize that moral virtue is central because it is defined as the habit of right desire. The habitual disposition to desire what one ought to desire—to intend the end one ought to seek and to choose aright the means for seeking it—is the very essence of a person's *ethos*, his admirable moral character.

Those who think that it is more important to consider a person's actions or the way that individuals conduct their lives forget that a person's moral character is not determined by this or that right or wrong action but only by the individual's habitual dispositions to act in this way or that. It is not activity as such that Aristotle dwells upon in his concern with living well, but only activity in accordance with virtue—with the habit of right desire.

For Aristotle, unlike most other moral philosophers, it is not doing good to others, acting righteously toward them or discharging one's social obligations, that is primary. It is desiring aright that is primary. All the rest follows from that.

When we turn from the realm of thought and theory to the realm of action and the practical, it is our appetites or desires that move or motivate us. In contemporary lingo, "motivation" is the word that replaces "desire" in naming our focal concern with what drives human beings to lead moral or immoral lives, or to form good or bad moral characters.

Single right or wrong actions, even such serious acts of depravity as murder, rape, deception, and treachery, are not the index to a person's moral character, that is, not unless they stem from a habitual right or wrong disposition or motivation to act in a certain way—in other words, right or wrong habits of desire.

In the sphere of conduct, a person can be moral but impractical (aiming at the right end, but choosing wrong, because ineffective, means); or practical but immoral (choosing effective or expedient means for the wrong end). In saying this, one is referring to the state of the individual's desires when one uses the words "moral" and "immoral" and one is referring to the success of the individual's actions when one uses the words "practical" and "impractical."

Turning from moral philosophy to Judeo-Christian moral theology, it is of interest to note the difference between the Ten Commandments and the catalogue of the seven cardinal or capital sins. The former forbid certain actions that ought not to be committed (murder, theft, adultery, and perjury); in only one instance do they proscribe a wrong desire (covetousness). In contrast, all of the seven capital sins are wrong habits of desire, not wrong actions. One can be forgiven for a wrong action, but never for a wrong habitual desire, such as greed, gluttony, avarice, sloth, anger, envy and pride.

The imperatives of action are prescriptions that state what one should or should not do. The imperatives of desire are prescriptions that state the ends or goals that one should or should not seek and the ways or means that one should or should not employ in order to attain them. The imperatives of desire concern the motivations engendered by our emotions or passions and the motivations engendered by our intellectual appetites, the habitual intentions or choices of our will.[2]

It should not be surprising that an ethics of desire, which is so uniquely Aristotelian, should also be an ethics in which the notion of *enough* plays a central role. In its concern with wrong desires, it might even be called an "ethics of enough."

---

2. While the distinction between two modes of desire is ethical, not psychological, the distinction between two kinds of human appetite—the sensitive appetite or sensual desires and the intellectual appetite or the acts of the will—is psychological, not ethical. I will return to the latter distinction at the end of Chapter 6.

In the second book of Aristotle's *Ethics*, which initiates his discussion of moral virtue, he introduces the notion of the mean—that which is neither too much nor too little in the sphere of desire, but just enough. There are goods to which the standard of the mean—of enoughness—does not apply, such as knowledge, understanding, wisdom, and even moral virtue itself as a good to be sought. But it certainly does apply, and most critically, when we deal with some of the wrong desires that are among our chief ethical problems.

I hope that I have now explained to my readers that this book is both a summation of my previous efforts to present Aristotelian moral philosophy to a contemporary audience and also a new departure, in principle as well as in detail,[3] by virtue of its focusing on desire as the central term in Aristotle's *Ethics*. I also hope that my readers will feel, as I do, that this approach is more pertinent than any other to the way most people think about the moral problems they confront.

—— 3 ——

In the preceding section I referred to the way most people think of the moral problems that confront them. I should have said most right-thinking persons, for there are many, perhaps even a majority among the educated and sophisticated, whose wrong thinking avoids or dismisses all moral problems. For them, there are only practical problems—problems of success or expediency in getting what they want. Let me deal first with the wrong thinking that leads to the

3. In my previous books and essays, I did not treat in detail or dwell upon what is wrong with desires for pleasure, money, or fame and power, and even with respect to wealth, health, and knowledge.

rejection of all moral problems. I will then, at the conclusion of this section, summarize the thinking that leads to their acknowledgment and its concern with their solution.

The most radical evasion of moral problems stems from the denial that value judgments about good and evil, right and wrong, together with prescriptions about what ought to be desired, can be either true or false in the way that applies to all statements of fact. Many of the persons who dismiss such judgments as sheer personal prejudice, expressions of unsupportable opinion, matters of individual taste about which there can be no argument, do not always realize that the only rational basis for their view lies in a theory of truth that is exclusively applicable to descriptive propositions.

Similarly, those who maintain that all value judgments and prescriptions are entirely subjective, relative to the temperament or upbringing of the individual person and to the circumstances of time and place, may not realize that this view of theirs is grounded in their being simplistic about desires. They incorrectly think that human desires are all of one mode. Yet desires differ from individual to individual. For everyone, there are few, if any, desires that remain constant or durable throughout a lifetime. What an individual likes or wants at one time, he or she may dislike or repel at another.

The statement by Hamlet, echoing Montaigne, that there is nothing good or evil but thinking makes it so, might be rephrased as follows: whatever opinion one holds about good and evil is nothing but an expression of what that individual does or does not desire, does or does not like. Hence the maxim *de gustibus non disputandum est* holds for all value judgments as merely matters of individual taste. Like beauty, which is thought to lie entirely in the eye of the beholder, so good and evil are thought to lie entirely in the appetites of those who make such evaluations.

Without explicitly realizing it, most persons who are relativists and subjectivists about values of every kind embrace a single-minded hedonism. When individuals place positive or negative values on whatever objects they are considering, they are simply saying what pleases or displeases them. Since what pleases one individual may not please another, and since what pleases a given individual at one time may not please him or her at another, their evaluations will vary from one individual to another, and from one time to another.

Another ground for subjectivism and relativism (of which those who espouse this view are seldom aware) is that, unlike other animals that have specific natures, it is claimed that human beings do not participate in a common or specific human nature.

As the existentialists put it, the nature of man is to have no nature. Without putting it so paradoxically, most social scientists, especially the cultural anthropologists, agree. Human beings may all have the same number of chromosomes, bones, or teeth, but they do not all have the same behavioral tendencies and traits.

In these respects, humans differ from tribe to tribe or from one ethnic group to another. As they differ in these respects, so do their values and their mores. What anthropologists call "the ethnocentric predicament" is the impossibility of making transcultural judgments. Individuals of one tribe or ethnic group cannot make objectively valid, adverse judgments about the mores—or the morals—that prevail in another tribe or ethnic group.

One point more must be added to this examination of the kind of thinking that enables individuals to live lives in which they are not confronted by moral problems, concerning the solution of which it is possible to argue and try to get at the truth. This point does not occur in the thinking of those who are innocent of the perplexities of modern philosophy, but it has perplexed philosophers since it was first stated by David Hume in the eighteenth century.

Hume observed that if we had complete knowledge of all matters of fact, we could not validly reason from that knowledge to a single prescriptive conclusion—a statement containing the words "ought" or "ought not." Hence such prescriptive judgments can have no rational basis whatsoever. This, of course, is another way of saying that there is no way to assess the truth or falsity of moral judgments. Hence they must be relegated to the realm of unsupportable opinion. Ethics, therefore, is not a science, not a body of verifiable knowledge.

Without being cognizant of the phrase "noncognitive ethics," which is the philosophical jargon for making this point, the laymen who avoid and dismiss moral problems would take comfort in the view that ethics or moral philosophy is not a respectable body of knowledge.

To summarize the thinking that leads to the acknowledgment of moral problems and to concern with their solution, I need only correct the errors in the thinking we have just considered. I can do that briefly by stating a series of propositions that are directly contrary to the views we have surveyed.

1. There are two kinds of truth, not just one kind. The truth of value judgments and of normative prescriptions is radically different from the kind of truth to be found in descriptive propositions about matters of fact. It consists in conformity with right desire, not, as in the case of

descriptive propositions, in their correspondence with the way things really are.

2. There are two modes of desires, not just one mode. There are acquired desires, differing from individual to individual, and there are natural desires, common to and inherent in all individuals who belong to the human species and so participate in one and the same human nature. The English names for these two radically different modes of desire are "wants" and "needs."

3. The evaluation of things as good or evil, and of desires and actions as right or wrong, is not reducible to a matter of taste—of liking or disliking, of being pleased or displeased.

4. Ethics or moral philosophy is a body of respectable knowledge, the conclusions of which are validly grounded in reasoning that combines true descriptive statements of fact (about what is or is not) with true prescriptions (about what ought or ought not to be desired and done). In such reasoning, the first principle is a self-evident prescriptive truth, a categorical imperative that does not rest on any knowledge of matters of fact.

————— 4 —————

Given this summary of the affirmations indispensable to acknowledging the existence of moral problems, those disposed to proceed with the reading of this book should be told what lies ahead for them.

In Chapter 1, we shall examine the meaning of "enough"—of too little, too much, and what lies between. Here the crucial question is whether enough is always relative to the temperament and circumstances of different individuals. Is there also a measure of enough that is the same for all individuals because they are all human?

In Chapter 2, the distinction between real and apparent goods will be explained in terms of the distinction between what is actually desired and what ought to be desired. Here also will be found an explanation of the distinction between right and wrong desires.

Chapter 3 will explore in detail desires that are wrong either because they are unlimited desires for real goods that are only limited goods or because they are unlimited desires for goods that are only apparent goods, not real goods.

Chapter 4 will explore in detail desires that are right either (a) because they are desires for real goods that are controlled by the consideration of neither too much nor too little, but just enough; (b) because they are desires for real goods that are unlimited goods; or (c) because they are desires for merely apparent goods that are innocuous, not noxious.

In Chapter 5, I shall identify the fundamental mistakes made in moral philosophy, with one exception in modern times, and also the modern philosophers who made them. The one exception is Plato and the Stoics in antiquity; but in modern times, Immanuel Kant made the same mistake. The other mistakes in moral philosophy made in modern times are made by David Hume, John Stuart Mill, and John Dewey.

In Chapter 6, I shall point out three factors that are required for the solution of moral problems when they are also practical problems—problems of action as well as of thought. Right thinking may give us the theoretical solution of moral problems, but by itself it is less than enough to solve those same problems practically.

What is required in addition is good fortune or good luck, the avoidance of incontinence in the conflict between reason and the passions (i.e., the conflict between right and wrong desires in the control of our actions), and a virtuous character, which is *not* produced by the intellectual understanding and affirmation of the truths of moral philosophy.

Finally, in an Epilogue, we will consider the question whether the principles and conclusions of ethics are or are not transcultural. We will find ourselves intellectually obliged to answer this question affirmatively or negatively in accordance with our earlier answer to the question of whether or not there is objectively valid truth in moral philosophy.

CHAPTER 1

THE ETHICS OF ENOUGH

1

W HO HAS NOT SAID OR HEARD someone else say "Enough is enough"? The statement is a tautology and, as such, uninstructive. But everyone knows what that idiomatic statement means: "That's enough, I don't want any more."

All of us have heard people say "That's not enough, that's too little, I want more" or "That's too much, I want less than that." And, perhaps, we are even acquainted with persons who have never said "That's enough" because they always want more.

If one were to ask the top executives of our major corporations, as they prepared for an annual board meeting, whether the gross income and profit margin of the year just closing was at a rate that satisfied them, so that the goal they set for the coming year was simply to duplicate it, their answer would be negative. A business that does not grow each year is likely not to remain stable, but rather to decline.

Few businessmen who have developed their business into a mature corporation that has managed to achieve what, for a given year, is a satisfactory gross income and profit, would be satisfied with a future in which that same satisfactory gross income and profit were repeated year after year. Why not? Is it true that what does not grow, necessarily declines? Is it folly in business ever to say "enough" when one has achieved a satisfactory gross income and margin of profit?

There are other aspects in the conduct of a business where the standard of enough is usually employed. Personnel officers, charged with hiring workers for different jobs, set a scale of remuneration for different levels of work. They know what it means to pay either too much or too little and they try to fix a rate that is just enough. Similarly, those who set prices for merchandise to be sold, try to estimate what existing market conditions will support. Other factors enter into the calculation: the sales volume desired and the margin of profit sought. When all the variables are considered, the price set should be just enough to achieve the goal in view, neither too much nor too little.

It is not only with respect to wages and prices that we have a general acquaintance with the standard of enough. That standard operates in many other walks of life. Everywhere there are traffic laws that regulate the speed of automobiles driving on the highways. The speed limit determines a velocity that is prohibited because it is more than enough for safety; and, in some states, driving too slowly on the freeway is also prohibited. There is a range of speeds—neither too slow nor too fast—that are regarded as safe; and though we are not given to using the word "enough" for the safe speeds, that, in fact, is what they are—just enough for safety in transportation.

Another area of life in which we generally recognize the

standard of enough is medical therapy. When physicians prescribe pills as a remedy, they almost always specify the quantity of each pill and the frequency with which they should be taken. The physician usually cautions us to be careful in this regard: "Don't fail to take them just as prescribed"—neither too little nor too much, but just enough for the therapeutic effect desired.

It is not a far step to go from moderation with respect to therapeutic remedies to moderation with respect to food and drink. Most of us regard anorexia and gluttony as the baleful or perilous extremes of too little and too much, between which there is a range of amounts that we are willing to settle for as just enough. Is it not also true that a house that is not a palace can have too many rooms for anyone's ordinary use as a home? That one's closet can have in it too many pairs of shoes, too many suits or dresses, too many overcoats for anyone's normal use? Is it not also true that those living in the temperate zones, who do not have any shelter at all that they can call their own, any clothing except the rags on their back, or any shoes on their feet, have too little?

Are the bare necessities of life enough? Are there not also certain amenities that everyone should enjoy in order for them to achieve a decent standard of living? Beyond that, are there not also certain things that are or should be regarded as luxuries because human beings can live well without having them?

All these questions and many more confront us the moment we think of anything to which the three estimates of too little, too much, and just enough apply. To whatever objects of desires these estimates apply, they also apply to our desires for them. If one can have too much of any purchasable commodity, it necessarily follows that the desire for that amount is an excessive desire—a desire for more than enough.

Are there any objects of desire to which these three estimates do not apply? Yes. I will consider them later in Chapter 4 where we are concerned with right desires. Here it is only necessary to point out that the familiar maxim of conduct—*moderation in all things*—is incorrect. It is a guideline for conduct only with respect to those things about which our desires should be moderate because, even if they are really good to possess, we can have too much of them. We can have too much of some good things, but not of all.

2

The important exception having been noted, it remains the case that in the ethics of right and wrong desire, the ethics of enough has crucial significance. One cannot go far in Aristotle's *Ethics* without discovering the importance of this point.

In Chapter 6 of Book II, after Aristotle has engaged in a preliminary exploration of moral virtue, he takes up the question of what is neither too much nor too little, but just enough. Moral virtue consists in habits of choice that aim at what is intermediate between excess and defect—in short, habits of choice that are properly moderated by reason and thereby aim at the mean.

Aristotle's discussion of what has come to be called "the golden mean" raises a serious problem for us. The mean, he says, is relative to the individual. A breakfast that is not excessive for a lumberjack who has worked in the woods two hours before he sits at the table would be too much for a sedentary worker who goes to breakfast on arising. Similarly, the number of rooms in the house of a junior government official would be too few for the uses to which senior officeholders must put their residence. Hence there would appear to be no absolute standard of enough that applies to all human beings, without variation from individual to individual.

Having said that "excess and defect are characteristic of vice, and the mean of virtue," Aristotle goes on as follows:

> Virtue, then, is a state of character concerned with choice, lying in a mean, i.e., the mean relative to us, this being determined by a rational principle, [or] by that principle by which the man of practical wisdom would determine it.

We manifest our desires in the choices we make. Moral virtue consists in the habit of right desire—in the stable and steadfast disposition to make right choices. Sometimes, but not always, these choices stem from moderate desires, aiming at the mean or what is intermediate between excess and defect. But that mean, Aristotle appears to say, is relative to the individual. What is enough for one individual, according to that individual's physique, temperament, and surrounding circumstances, may be either too much or too little for another individual, differing in physical constitution, temperamental disposition, and conditions of life.

Hence when reason—in the form of prudence or practical wisdom—operates to determine what is just enough, what is moderate in amount or intermediate between excess and defect, it must take into consideration all the individual differences that make the mean, or what is just enough, different for different individuals.

How, then, can we avoid the relativism that asserts there

is no absolute standard of right desire, a standard not relative to individual differences and the varying circumstances of time and place? If there is an acceptable answer to this question, it must lie in the sameness of the human nature in which all human beings participate equally, for no person is more or less human than another.

The sameness of the human nature in which all human beings equally participate does not eliminate individual differences entirely, but it does limit the extent to which they occur. One example will suffice to make this clear. With respect to stature, no mature human being is taller than eight feet or shorter than three feet; heavier than four hundred pounds or lighter than fifty pounds. The numbers I have used may not be statistically precise but they nevertheless suggest the limited range within which individual differences vary.

The sameness of human nature, physically, biologically, and psychologically, sets a limit to the range within which individual differences can occur in any trait. Accordingly, the line that runs from the extreme of defect to the extreme of excess is defined by a point that is absolutely too little for everyone to a point that is absolutely too much for everyone. What is intermediate or the mean between these two extremes is not a single point on that line which is enough for everyone. Instead, there is a circle in the middle of the line which encloses all the degrees of enough for everyone. What is a degree of enough for one individual may be too much or too little for another, but what is enough for everyone, varying in degree, falls within this circle that is intermediate or the mean between what is absolutely too much or absolutely too little for any human being, precisely because they are all equally human.

—— 3 ——

The sameness of human nature, in which we all participate, provides another escape from the relativism that appears to follow from the mean's being determined relative to the attributes and circumstances of the individual. Individuals do not differ from each other in all their desires. There are two modes of human desire: (a) desires which are the same for all human beings because they are inherent in human nature and so are natural desires, and (b) desires that individuals acquire from the way in which they are nurtured or as a result of the circumstances that impinge upon them in the course of their lives. The natural desires are common human desires; the acquired desires differ widely from individual to individual.

Two English words—"needs" and "wants"—are the names for these two modes of desire. When they are not misused, as they are by children, who frequently say they "need" what they should say they "want," these two words have great significance for the ethics of enough. We certainly can want too much or too little of something that is really good for us, but we can never need too much or too little of it.

Consider our basic biological needs—our natural need for food, for drink, for sleep, for shelter, and for clothing. In all these instances of things our human nature needs because we cannot survive without them, we may want more or less than we need (pathologically, abnormally, viciously); but our need can only be for enough—neither too little nor too much.

The human need for these biologically indispensable

goods will fall within the circle of the mean (i.e., the degrees of enough with respect to which individuals differ). Though there are degrees of individual difference with respect to needs, the needs of every human being will fall within that circle. In that qualified sense, all human needs are the same and what is enough for any human being is enough for all.

The controlling insight can be stated as follows: enough of any good is that amount of it which serves the end that ought to be sought by everyone as the object of their right desire.

CHAPTER 2

REAL AND APPARENT GOODS

1

As we have seen, one way in which desires go wrong is wanting more than you need—more than enough for any human being regardless of individual or racial differences, differences in nurture and in external circumstances. But that is not the only way in which our appetites can go wrong. We may also want what only appears to be good, but is not really good for any human being under any circumstances.

The distinction already made between needs and wants as two distinct modes of desire is indispensable now to understanding the differences between real and apparent goods. To see that this is so, one should entertain the supposition that all our desires are of the same sort—all wants, no needs—all acquired desires that differ from individual to individual, as well as from time to time, and vary with variations in the circumstances.

On this supposition, would it not follow that each of us would call good whatever it was that we happened to desire at a particular time and under particular circumstances?

That which we actually desired at a given moment would, at that moment, appear good to us. At some other time and under other circumstances, we might not like it and desire it. We might even be disappointed by it later after we managed to get what we desired, or even regret ever having wanted it. But at the time we wanted it, it would, in fact, have appeared good to us. It could not have been otherwise.

Hence if all desires were wants and all goods were merely apparently so, changing from time to time for the same individual and differing from individual to individual, the only persons who might call a desire wrong would be persons who actually desired it earlier and then later thought it a wrong desire, wishing that they had not attained what they had wanted. They might say that they had made a mistake in wanting something that they later did not like or enjoy having. But no other individual could make that judgment. No one else could say they were wrong in their earlier desire. In short, there would be no objectively valid and universally applicable criterion for distinguishing between right and wrong desires. All goods would be apparent, none real.

2

What, then, makes some desires objectively and universally right and others wrong? I must repeat what I have said before on this subject. The obvious answer to the question is that right desire consists in desiring what everyone ought to desire. But what should every human being desire? That which is really good for all of them in accordance with their common human nature.

One more question remains. What is really good for all

human beings in accordance with their common human nature? If it is not something that only appears good because it is actually wanted, then it must be something that satisfies a natural need that all of us are born with; as, for example, our need for food and drink. No animal can long survive being deprived of these goods. It is precisely because they are indispensable goods, that they are really good.

The difference between real and apparent goods can be perceived in another way. In the case of apparent goods, the actual desires that each of us has causes the objects actually desired to appear good to us at the time we want them. In the case of real goods, the order is reversed. We ought to desire them, whether we actually do or not, because they are really good for us.

What makes anything appear good to us is the fact that we actually want it. What makes anything really good for us is the fact that we naturally need it. But we may not want what we need. We may not actually desire what we ought to desire. The fact that something is really good for us is the reason—the *only* reason—why we ought to desire it.

In the seventeenth century, Benedict de Spinoza asked the question whether we called something good because we desired it or desired it because it was good. His question cannot be clearly answered without first distinguishing two senses in which the good is the desirable and the desirable is the good: (a) the sense in which something is desirable if it is actually desired, and (b) the sense in which something is desirable if it ought to be desired. Apparent goods are good in sense (a); real goods, good in sense (b).

In the one case (a), goodness is attributed to the objects. Calling something good because it is actually desired is an *extrinsic* denomination. In the other case (b), goodness inheres in the object. Calling it good is an *intrinsic* denomination.

It is, of course, possible for us to want what we need. Then the needed real good will also appear good to us. We not only ought to desire it; we also actually desire it. But it is equally possible for us not to want what we need or to want what we do not need. We may not actually desire what is really good for us, or actually desire what is not really good for us.

The only wants that are intrinsically right desires for real goods are the wants identical with our needs. When we actually want what we naturally need, then our wants are right desires. But they are not acquired as all other wants are. They come into existence by an act of will—an act of the intellectual appetite, after rational deliberation, discipline, and decision to want what we ought to desire.

In the sphere of our desires, the distinction between right and wrong is applicable only to our wants. Wants can be right or wrong, but needs are always right desires, never wrong. How could any living organism, brute animal or human, need something that was really bad for it? That is just as absurd as needing either more or less than enough.[1]

----- 3 -----

We cannot go immediately from understanding what has just been said to a simple statement about right and wrong

1. If the need is truly a natural desire, inherent in human nature, the absurdity of saying that our natures have appetitive inclinations toward things that are injurious to them is clear. But we are cognizant of the fact that those suffering from drug or alcohol addiction genuinely need injurious substances. Their substance abuse arises from a craving that is a pathological, not a natural, need and requires therapy.

desires in the case of our wants. It is not sufficient to say that wanting what we need—things that are really good for us—is right desire. With respect to both our needs and our wants, there are further complications to be considered.

In the first place, not all our human needs are of the biological sort already mentioned. They are not all needs that we share with other animal organisms—not all needs for real goods that we cannot live without. In the case of all other animals, there is no distinction between living and living well, but in the case of humankind, living—mere subsistence—falls short of living well.

For a human being, merely to subsist or survive is not to live a decent human life—one that is characteristic of the human species and of no other. As food, drink, and sleep are necessities of life itself, so sufficient wealth, freedoms of various sorts, loves and friendships, knowledge far beyond anything needed for survival and, beyond knowledge, understanding and wisdom, are needed for a good life—for living well as opposed to just living. These are, for human beings, real goods in the same sense that food, drink, and sleep are real goods.

In the second place, we must distinguish between primary natural needs and those that are secondary and instrumental. The primary natural needs are those that are inherent in human nature and so are the same for all human beings everywhere and at all times. Having a capacity for knowledge, man has a natural need for it. As Aristotle said, "man by nature desires to know."

To acquire knowledge, human beings do not need schools as now constituted and operated. At other times and under other circumstances, the need for knowledge was served by parental instruction, indoctrination and discipline by the elders of the tribe, pedagogues and tutors, and so on. There are many different means to serve the acquisition of knowledge by the young. At different times and under different circumstances, each of these different means may be required to implement the acquisition of the real good needed.

These secondary and instrumental needs can be called "natural" only in the sense that they are means for implementing needs that are natural. They themselves are not natural in the sense of being inherent in human nature and so common to all human beings everywhere and at all times.

Keeping this distinction in mind helps us answer the question often asked: "Do not natural needs change from time to time and with variations in the surrounding circumstances?" The answer is both no and yes. No, primary natural needs never vary. Yes, the instrumental needs that we call "natural" because they are needed to implement our natural desires, do change.

In our present society, people think schools are needed; that was not always the case. In our urban society, people think that public transportation is needed to serve the need to earn a living by those who live at a distance from their place of work. That was not the case in tribal life or in rural agricultural communities. Health is a primary natural need, but it is only in an environment being polluted by the effects of advanced technology that we now need, secondarily and instrumentally, environmental protection for the care of our health.

When the word "need" is used with reference to whatever may be needed to implement our natural desires, we must remember that, unlike our primary natural needs, the secondary instrumental needs are variable. New needs come into existence; needs that once existed disappear. Such variation in needs violates the sense of the word "natural" when it is applied to primary needs. The secondary needs can be called "natural" only in the sense that the goods needed serve to implement genuinely natural needs.

In the third place, it is a mistake to think that wanting what is not needed is always wrong desire. While it is true that wanting what is needed is always right desire, the apparent goods we want but do not need fall into two groups.

On the one hand, they may be innocuous apparent goods; on the other hand, they may be noxious. Clearly, wanting noxious apparent goods is wrong desire. Wanting innocuous apparent goods is right desire, but not in the same sense that wanting real goods is right desire. The latter is right in the sense of being *permissible*; the former, in the sense of being *obligatory*.

What makes an apparent good innocuous or noxious? Something that we want is innocuous if our wanting it or the degree to which we want it does not prevent or seriously impede our attaining one or more of the real goods we need. Noxious apparent goods do just that. They displace or attenuate our desires for the real goods we ought to want; or they come into conflict with such desires and interfere with our wanting the real goods we need. Hence, we can correctly say that wanting apparent goods that are innocuous is permissible right desire and wanting apparent goods that are noxious is wrong desire.

----- 4 -----

The distinction between ends and means that is involved in the distinction between primary natural needs and the needs called secondary and instrumental brings us to still one more criterion for judging desires to be wrong. To desire what is merely a means as if it were not a means but *the* end is wrong desire.

In the order of means and ends, there are (a) some objects that are to be desired merely as means and never as ends, and (b) some objects that are to be desired as ends as well as means to further ends. The third possibility is (c) an object of desire that is desired wholly for its own sake and not for the sake of anything else. Such an object of desire is never desired as *an* end, as are all the objects that are desired both as ends and as means. On the contrary, it is desired as *the* end—the last or final end for which all other things are desired as means.

It may be asked why there must be a final or ultimate end; and, if so, what desirable good has this status.

To the first question the answer is that, in the sphere of desire, we begin by desiring ends. That precedes our desiring means, just as our desiring goods precedes the actions involved in obtaining them. Hence if the series of means and ends had no last end, it would also have no beginning. Every end being a means to some further end, neither desire or action could ever begin. There must be something regarded as the last and ultimate end, which is the first principle of both desiring and acting, if desire and action are to occur.

What desirable good has the status of a final and ultimate end? Obviously, it must be something that leaves nothing more to be desired.

Desired how? Needed or wanted? Is the final end something that everyone actually desires or something that everyone ought to desire? As I have already pointed out, one criterion for judging desire to be wrong is desiring what is a means as if it were the final end. What we are concerned with here is right desire for the ultimate end that everyone ought to desire. The only desirable object that omits nothing that ought to be desired is that whole the parts of which are all the real goods that ought to be desired; in short, the *totum bonum.*

Here, then, is the only self-evident principle in the sphere of desire, the only truly categorical imperative. *We ought to desire everything really good for us and nothing else.*

A self-evident truth is a truth the opposite of which is unthinkable and undeniable. We can test the self-evidence of the categorical imperative just stated by trying to think that we ought to desire what is really bad for us, or trying to think that we ought not to desire what is really good for us.

The two phrases "really good" and "ought to be desired" coimplicate each other in the same way that the words "part" and "whole" coimplicate each other in the axiom about finite wholes; namely, that a finite whole is greater than any of its parts and that each part is less than the whole to which it belongs. No other understanding of the relation of parts and wholes is possible.

With respect to each of the goods that is a component of the *totum bonum* (the whole that includes all real goods), there are imperatives stating that we ought to seek them, but these imperatives are conditional or hypothetical, not categorical. For example, that we ought to seek health, wealth, liberty, or knowledge follows from the principle that we ought to seek everything that is really good. But in each case the conclusion requires another premise, namely, that as a matter of fact our human nature is such that inherent in it is the need for health, wealth, liberty, and knowledge, and so these are real goods that ought to be desired.

In each case, it is the factual premise that makes the imperative hypothetical or conditional (i.e., only *if* some wealth is needed and hence is really good for us, ought we to desire it). Only with regard to the *totum bonum* is the imperative categorical; for no factual considerations of any kind enter into the self-evident truth that we ought to seek everything that is really good for us.

Does this mean that the final and ultimate end is the same for all human beings? No, because in addition to the real goods that we are all obliged to seek, there are innocuous apparent goods that each of us is permitted to seek.

The final end for one individual will be the same as the final end for every other individual only with respect to its component real goods. Since individuals differ with respect to the innocuous apparent goods that we are permitted to seek, the final end that individuals do, in fact, actually seek will have components that differ from individual to individual as well as components that are the same for all.

—— 5 ——

Everyone uses the word "happiness" for that which leaves nothing more to be desired and which, therefore, is the final or ultimate end of all desire. That everyone uses the word in this sense is attested by the fact that no one is able to complete the sentence "I want to be happy because . . ." No one can think of happiness as a means to something beyond itself. No one can think of a reason for wanting to be happy.

But, while this is true, it is also true that people use the word "happiness" in two quite different senses. Most people, including many who in modern times call themselves philosophers, use the word for a psychological state of contentment that consists in getting what they want, i.e., for the satisfaction of all their wants, wrong or right desires.

Happiness, thus conceived, is experienceable and enjoyable. It varies, as apparent goods do, from individual to individual. For any one individual, it can be attained or not attained from day to day—attained in one period of life, but not in another. We are at one time contented as a result of getting what at that time we want, while at another time we are discontented because at that time our wants are frustrated.

When happiness is so conceived, there is nothing right or wrong about differing individual pursuits of it, for there is nothing objectively and universally right or wrong in the sphere of desire if all desires are wants and there are no desires that are needs.

However, there is another meaning of happiness to be found in antiquity, especially in Aristotle's *Ethics*. This happiness is conceived as a whole life well lived by reason of the fact that it involves the successive, not simultaneous, attainment of everything that a human being needs, everything that is really good.

This is the ethical, not psychological, conception of happiness. Happiness so conceived is not experienceable, enjoyable, or attainable at any moment in one's life. It is the final end all of us are morally obliged to seek, whether we actually do or not.

The categorical imperative that we ought to seek everything that is really good for us expresses our obligation to try to live well and to make morally good lives for ourselves. On this ethical conception of happiness, the pursuit of happiness is not only a right but a duty. The natural rights related to happiness are rights to life, liberty, and to everything that anyone needs in order to discharge the obligation to pursue happiness, but only, of course, if the state's duty to secure such rights is within the power of its government to discharge.[2]

We can now return to the point of departure of the foregoing analysis of the final and ultimate end in the sphere of desire. It started by noting that desires can be judged wrong if they convert anything that is a means (whether it be a real good or an apparent good) into a final end. To this it must now be added that the only right desire for an end that is final and ultimate is the desire for the happiness we are morally obliged to pursue throughout the course of our lives. To see anything else as a final and ultimate end is either to convert means into ends or to conceive happiness as the psychological state of contentment that results from our getting the apparent goods we want. In either case, the pursuit of happiness is motivated by wrong desires.

---

2. If, for example, moral virtue is among the goods needed to pursue happiness, no state or government can facilitate the acquisition of moral virtue by its citizens. But it can do so with respect to such real goods as wealth, health, liberty, and so on. These are among the needed real goods to which citizens have a natural, human, and unalienable right and that a just government has an obligation to secure. This holds true only if the ethical conception of happiness prevails. On the psychological conception of happiness, no government could have the duty to facilitate the pursuit of happiness, because citizens would come into conflict with one another with regard to their unlimited wants for apparent goods. The pursuit of happiness would be competitive, not cooperative, and no government could prevent some from failing while others succeeded.

CHAPTER 3

WRONG DESIRES

Pleasure, Money, Fame and Power

1

THE BIBLICAL STATEMENT that the love of money is the root of all evil does not assert that money is undesirable or that, desired for its purchasing power, it cannot be properly esteemed as a useful means. What, then, is the message? What is the root from which all wrong desires stem?

The fault common to all wrong desires is the mistake of treating as an end desired for its own sake and for nothing beyond or outside itself that which, for any one of three reasons, cannot legitimately serve as the end of all human striving.

The root from which all wrong desires spring is three-pronged: either (a) the wrong desire is for something that, while really good and needed, is only a partial good (a component part of the *totum bonum*), yet is desired inordinately as if it were the only good, the whole good; or (b) something that, while good as a means, is a limitless good for those who desire it as an ultimate end; or (c) something that, though it may appear to be good when actually desired, is an apparent good that is noxious rather than innocuous.

The prime examples of this threefold classification of the objects of wrong desires are (a) pleasure, (b) money, and (c) fame and power. What is true of pleasure as a real but only partial and limited good is true of other partial goods, such as health, wealth, freedom, and even knowledge, none of which can be rightly desired inordinately as if it were by itself the ultimate or complete good. But pleasure, much more frequently than any of these other partial goods, is the object of wrong desire when it is desired as the only good, and as the ultimate goal of one's striving.

Another summary account of wrong desires stresses placing one's happiness—that which leaves nothing more to be desired—in something that, while really good as a component of happiness, is not the *totum bonum*; or placing it in something that, if sought and attained, will impede or frustrate the pursuit of happiness.

Pleasure, money, and fame and power are goods, real or apparent, that can be attained and possessed by knaves and villains as well as by the virtuous. That by itself indicates that they can all be wrongly desired. It also shows, at least in the case of pleasure and money, that they can sometimes be rightly desired. However, that is not the case when we come to fame and power, especially when they are desired for their own sake.

—— 2 ——

Let us begin our consideration of wrong desires with pleasure.

The understanding of pleasure as a physiological and psychological phenomenon is much more complicated and difficult than the consideration of the grounds that determine whether our desires for pleasure are right or wrong; or, since a desire for pleasure can be right as well as wrong, the criteria for telling which, in any case, it is.

In the physiology of sensation, the organs of the different and distinct sensory faculties are plotted corporeally. Along with the organs of sight, hearing, and smell, there are the four organs of the cutaneous senses—the sensitive apparatus for being aware of heat, cold, pressure, and pain. These organs are mainly to be found in the epidermis of the body, though some are also found in the viscera. What will come as a surprise to many readers is that there are no sensitive nerve endings for pleasure.

Speaking in neurological terms, there is no *sense* of pleasure. Yet, most of us speak and think of pleasure and pain as opposites, in the same way that the senses of heat and cold are opposites. A moment's further consideration will remind us that we often use the word "pain" to refer to the feeling that results from the deprivation or loss of something we desire, and not for a sensory experience of the sort we have when a sharp point is inflicted on the surface of our bodies. That is purely sensory pain, as the pain of loss is not. Thus it may be that when we think of pleasure and pain as contrary opposites, that contrariety, which is not in the sphere of sense, must be assigned to another psychological sphere.

We may have to use the loose and ambiguous word "feeling" for that other sphere of experience, which is strictly not sensory. Psychologists sometimes use the technical word "affect" and sometimes use the phrase "affective tone or quality" for this element in our experience. They speak of certain sensations as having a *pleasant* or an *unpleasant* affective tone.

This consideration of the affects may account for our incorrect attribution of pleasure to the sphere of sense, for certain cutaneous sensations of pleasure, such as tickling the skin, or of hot and cold, when they are not too extreme, are experienced by many as pleasant. Though it may be regarded as pathological, the experience even of sensory pain may be felt by some persons as pleasant. When we say that the masochist gets pleasure from the suffering of pain, the pain referred to is sensory but the pleasure referred to is not; instead, it is pleasurable only in respect to its pleasantness as an affect or feeling.

This leads us to the most important distinction with regard to pleasures and pains. When we say we are pleased or displeased, or that we take pleasure or find pleasure in something, we are using the word "pleasure" for the experience of satisfaction that we have when a desire is fulfilled or requited. So, too, we use the word "pain" for the dissatisfaction or frustration we experience when we do not succeed in getting something that we desire. Here pleasure and pain do not signify objects of desire, but rather the satisfaction or frustration of desire.

It would be confusingly redundant to refer to the satisfaction of a desire as if it were also an object of desire. For example, when, parched on a hot day, we desire a cool drink to slake our thirst, the cool drink may give us a sensation that has a pleasant affective tone, but the satisfaction that results from slaking our thirst is not itself an object of our desire. That was the cool drink itself; and the experienced pleasantness of that cool drink is not the same as the experienced satisfaction of our getting it.

The reason why all of these distinctions, however cumbersome they may be, are of such great importance is that the moral problems concerning pleasure must always focus on pleasure—or for that matter pain—solely as objects of desire, and never on pleasure and pain as the experienced satisfaction or frustration of desire. The latter accompanies all our desires—the desires that we have for the widest variety of objects, among which pleasure and pain will be found.

The Epicureans or hedonists in moral philosophy, who make the serious mistake of asserting that pleasure is the only good, make this mistake by failing to distinguish between pleasure as object of desire and pleasure as satisfaction of desire. It is true that pleasure is attendant upon all desires when they are satisfied, but not all desires have pleasure as their sole object.

Both Plato and Aristotle refute the error of hedonism by asking whether it is better—and wiser—to desire both pleasure and wisdom (as objects) than to seek pleasure as the only desirable object. The wiser man does, of course, realize more pleasure when he succeeds with both objects than the person who succeeds only with pleasure as an object of desire, but the greater pleasure of the wiser man is pleasure as the satisfaction of desire.

When this is clearly understood, it solves John Stuart Mill's problem about the pleasures of Socrates as being greater than and preferable to the pleasures of a pig. The greater amount of pleasure here is the satisfaction of more right desires, the desire for both wisdom and pleasure, not just for pleasure alone as the only object of desire.

In addition, it helps to understand the fact that successful criminals may, during the period of their success, be thoroughly pleased by their achievements, though their immoral conduct is motivated by wrong desires—desires for objects that they either ought not desire or ought not seek in the way that they do. If pleasure were the only object of desire, or if pleasure as object of desire were not distinguished from pleasure as satisfaction of desire, it would be impossible to say that there are good and bad pleasures, or that morally virtuous and morally vicious human beings can both experience pleasure.

Epicurus may have been a hedonist, thinking that pleasure is the only good and pain the only evil, but John Stuart Mill, in his essay *Utilitarianism*, is not an Epicurean. Though he explicitly calls himself one, he tries at the same time to ameliorate the individious connotations that attach to the term Epicureanism.

Mill does this by using the word "pleasure" only sometimes for an object of desire, but much more frequently as signifying the satisfaction of morally approved desires, including the benevolent desire for the welfare of others as well as selfish desires for one's own well-being. He also does this without explicitly acknowledging the basic distinction between pleasure as object and pleasure as satisfaction of desire.

In consequence, Mill's conception of happiness as the maximization of pleasure conceals his agreement with Aristotle's conception of happiness as the *totum bonum* (a whole life enriched by the possession of all real goods, including pleasure among them). In addition, if he had understood pleasure as an object of desire distinct from pleasure as the satisfaction of desire, he would not have been confronted with the insoluble problem of a conflict between two ultimate ends—the happiness of the individual and the general happiness of all mankind.[1]

When Saint Augustine summarizes his conception of hap-

---

1. See the further criticism of these serious defects in Mill's *Utilitarianism* in Chapter 5, Section 4. It should be added here that the correction of these serious defects would reduce Mill's *Utilitarianism* to a poor, because inadequate, restatement of fundamental truths in Aristotle's *Ethics*.

piness as a whole life in which all desires are satisfied, he adds the provision that nothing be desired amiss; in other words, that none of the satisfactions involved be attendant upon success in achieving objects wrongly desired.

This brings us back to the main point we must consider (in fact, the only point to be considered) with respect to the desire for pleasure: By what criteria should we judge certain pleasures as objects of wrong desires or as objects desired in a wrong way? In other words, when are we rightly and when are we wrongly pleased to attain the pleasures we seek as objects of desire?[2]

From this point on, let us confine our attention to pleasure as an object of desire. With this restriction, pain as an object of desire is always sensual pain, but pleasure as an object of desire is never a sensation of any sort. It is always the affective tone or quality of some sensual experience, such as the sensual experience of tickling or rubbing, the sensual experience of hot and cold, or the sensual experiences in other spheres, such as our experience of taste, smell, or sexual activity. When we find ourselves speaking of higher and lower pleasures, let us remember that we have shifted our attention from pleasure as an object of desire to pleasure as the satisfaction of desire, the higher pleasures being aesthetic or intellectual pleasures—the enjoyment of beauty or the enjoyment of learning in the process of knowing and understanding.

2. In everyday speech, when we say we are pleased or that something gives us pleasure, we are referring to the satisfaction experienced in the possession of the objects desired. Similarly, when we say we are pained in the sense of being displeased, we are referring to our deprivation, lack, or loss of objects desired. Pleasures and pains in this sense of possession or deprivation may, of course, be morally good or bad according to the goodness or badness of the objects desired or the way in which they are desired. This explains how morally vicious persons can be as thoroughly pleased with their successes as morally virtuous persons.

When pleasure is a sensual object (not as a sensation, but as the pleasant affective tone or quality of some sensual experience), it can be rightly desired only if the following conditions are fulfilled: (1) if it is desired as one among the real goods that human beings naturally need and not as the only good; (2) if it is desired with moderation and not inordinately, that is, neither too much nor too little, but just enough; and (3) if the pursuit of such pleasure does not involve any injury to others. In other words, an individual's pursuit of pleasure as an object of desire must not impede or in any other way detract from the pursuit of other real goods needed for his or her happiness or deprive others of the real goods needed for the pursuit of their happiness.

These three criteria tell us at once the conditions under which pleasure is wrongly desired as a sensual object: (1) when it is desired as if it were the sole object, or as if it were the total content of a happy life; (2) when it is inordinately or immoderately desired, in other words, when more than enough pleasure is desired; and (3) when the desire for pleasure results in the deprivation, for oneself or others, of real goods they need to constitute the *totum bonum* which is the common human good—the happiness that is the same for all human beings.

Most of the wrong desires for sensual pleasure fall into the sphere of eating, drinking, sleeping, playing, and sexual activity. It is with respect to such pleasures that the aspect of moral virtue called temperance is concerned. Habitual gluttony, drunkenness, sloth, brutality in the treatment of other human beings, and lasciviousness or unrestrained concupiscence are the vicious dispositions that lead to intemperance in the desire for sensual pleasure.

Intemperance is not limited to habitual overindulgence in sensual pleasure. It includes the opposite excess—abstemiousness with respect to pleasure as an object of desire, too little or none as opposed to too much or all. Asceticism may be advocated by moral theology, but even on that plane it cannot be accomplished except supernaturally—with the help of God's grace. On the purely natural plane, the abstemiousness of the person who shuns the pleasure of food, drink, sleep, play, or sex is as intemperate as the overindulgence of the drunkard, the playboy, or the libertine.

On the natural plane, moral theology does not command asceticism in the spheres of food, drink, or play. But a problem is raised by certain moral theologians in the realm of Christianity with respect to sex. They conceive chastity as the engagement by married persons in connubial sexual activity for only one purpose—the procreation and care of offspring. They exclude, as unchaste, sexual activity for the sensual pleasure that is thereby enjoyed.

Any sexual activity that is not reproductive in aim, they regard as perverse, because unnatural. While it is true that nonhuman animals generally or for the most part engage instinctively in copulation only when that sexual act works for the reproduction of the species, there are grounds for questioning whether, in this respect, human beings do not differ remarkably from all other animals.[3]

—— **3** ——

Let us turn next to money and to that with which it is often incorrectly identified, wealth.

3. On this point, see Note 1 in Appendix I. See also, in Appendix I, Note 2 with regard to other considerations relevant to right and wrong desire in the sphere of sexual behavior, especially in view of what in this century has been called "the sexual revolution"—that departure from Puritanism in its degree of permissiveness.

Clearly, money as an object of desire is not something that is naturaly needed, such as food and drink, clothing and shelter. It is, therefore, not a real, but only an apparent good—something deemed good simply because it is in fact desired. Yet that desire may be a permissible, even if it is not a right, desire—even if it is not something that ought to be desired.

Money is wrongly desired when it is desired as an end in itself and not purely as a means. In the myth of Midas, we have the classic example of a person who wished everything he touched to be turned into gold, only to discover too late how lethally wrong that desire was.

Consider the pathological case of the miser who deprives himself of economic goods that ensure the comforts and conveniences of life. He takes inordinate pleasure in fondling the gold he has accumulated. For the sake of that pleasure in the touch of money, he does not spend it for things that human beings need.

Money may be desired as the economic equivalent of real wealth, which means desired for its purchasing power. Real wealth, in contrast, consists in consumable goods and services and also in all the instrumentalities which, with the exception of human labor, can implement the production of goods and services.

When we recognize that money is valuable only for its purchasing power—to pay rent, insurance premiums, and other forms of debt, and to buy things that are either necessary for subsistence, or that provide life's comforts and conveniences, its amenities and luxuries—we are then confronted with the problem of right and wrong desire for real wealth.

Aristotle's summary formulation of the condition of living well—that *living well consists in a life lived in accordance with virtue and accompanied by a moderate possession of wealth*—indicates that, in his view, wealth is an indispensable component of the *totum bonum*. It is one of the real goods to which every human has a natural right.

It follows that wealth can be rightly desired, but only if it is desired in moderation and not to excess or inordinately. Why should there be a limit to the amount of wealth that can be rightly desired? There are many answers to this question. Let us consider some of them.

The first and most obvious reason for a limitation on the amount of wealth that can be rightly desired is that desire for wealth without limit, as if it were the only real good or the supreme good, interferes with, impedes, or frustrates the attainment of other real goods that are not only needed components of the *totum bonum*, but also much more valuable for a good life than wealth is.

Wealth is good only as a means, but knowledge and understanding, for example, or friendships and freedom, are good in themselves as well as constituent means to a good life. Hence, when the desire for wealth is inordinate or without limit, it tends to defeat the pursuit of happiness. It undermines the effort to lead a good life. It thus becomes a prototype of wrong desire, in the same way that the desire for excessive sensual pleasure is a prototype of wrong desire.

John Locke gives us other reasons for limiting the desire for wealth. He contends that no one should appropriate more real wealth than he can consume or put away for later consumption. He should not hoard that which, not used, will perish and be wasted. Another limitation that Locke places on the accumulation of wealth is that no one should appropriate so much of it that not enough is left for others to appropriate what they need.

Both of these limitations, in Locke's view, are rendered

inapplicable when money is introduced into any economy. For money can be hoarded greedily without violating the injunction that spoilage and waste should be avoided; and, though natural resources are limited in their amount, there would appear to be no limit to the amount of money that can be made available for appropriation.

Aristotle made the same observation centuries earlier in antiquity. "Men seek after a better notion of riches and of the art of getting wealth than the mere acquisition of coin, and they are right . . . for there is no bound to the riches which spring from this art of wealth-getting." The wrong desire for more houses than one can put to use, more shoes than one can wear, more food than one can eat and remain healthy, is obvious to most reasonable persons; but since money can be hoarded for a future (often unspecified) use, it is more difficult to set limits to the amount that can be rightly desired.

Nevertheless, for most of us, the word "greed" is disapprobative, even though we cannot condemn greed as easily in relation to the accumulation of money as we can in the case of those whose desires appear to us to be excessive with respect to the acquisition of consumable goods—more than anyone needs or can put away unused without spoilage or waste.

The misuse of money is the root of wrong desire with regard to wealth. This becomes evident by considering a barter economy conducted without money as an instrument of exchange. Inordinate desire for the possession of consumable goods, beyond the limits of usefulness set by nature, would be readily recognized as pathological motivation.

In such an economy, it would be easy to draw the line between greedy persons and those who virtuously sought a limited amount of wealth as an indispensable condition of living a good life. Only when money enters the picture does that line become hazy or obfuscated. That results from the accumulation of money without the limitation imposed by converting an amount of money into the amount of consumable goods and services that are needed for a good life.

The matter is further complicated by the consideration of what is enough in the sphere of real wealth. Is that middle ground between excess and defect relative to the individual, and so different for different persons? Or can we say that there is an amount of real wealth that is too little for any human being to be able to lead a good life; or an amount that is too much for anyone?

Money can be spent in the wrong pursuit of sensual pleasures to excess. To lead the life of a playboy involves an undue expenditure of money. Thus one wrong desire leads to another. Similarly, those who wrongly desire fame and power may seek an excess of money to spend for the satisfaction of that aim.

In the catalogue of human vices, greed and avarice should be as clearly recognizable as gluttony and insobriety. That, I think, would be the case were it not for the way in which the accumulation of money evades the limitations that most human beings for the most part accept when it comes to food and drink.

----- 4 -----

In this ignominious triad of pleasure, money, and fame and power, only fame and power are, for the most part, objects of wrong desires. There may be one or two exceptions to this statement, but in the main fame and power are only apparent goods and ought not to be desired for their own sake or as a means to happiness. They are not components of the *totum bonum*.

In contrast, pleasure is a real good and can be desired rightly in moderation and as a constituent of happiness. The same is true of wealth. As for money, which is, like fame and power, only an apparent good, it falls within the class of apparent goods permissible to desire, if the desire for money does not conflict with attaining real goods that ought to be desired.

In dealing with fame, we must bear in mind the distinction between fame and honor. A virtuous person is an honorable person, a person who ought to be honored by the community in which he or she lives. But the virtuous person does not seek honor, being secure in his or her own self-respect. Lack of honor does not in any way detract from the efficacy of moral virtue as an indispensable operative means in the pursuit of happiness.

Virtuous persons may be considered fortunate if their virtue is recognized and publicly applauded. Being honored for one's virtue is a gift of good fortune and like other gifts of fortune it may be an ingredient in the good life. But the misfortune of not being honored is not a major obstacle to living well, as are poverty, the lack of liberty, or the loss of health.

These other goods of fortune are rightly desired by virtuous persons who recognize them to be goods not entirely within their power to achieve. While this is true of honor also, virtuous persons may enjoy being honored, but they are under no moral obligation to seek it. They may think themselves dishonored if others do not pay them the respect that accords with their self-respect.

The distribution of honor raises questions of justice; in fact, it is thought to be one of the chief problems of distributive justice. For those who hold that honor and fame are distinct in principle, this is the clear mark of their difference. Justice does not require that fame be proportionate to virtue.

Those totally lacking in virtue may achieve fame as readily as, perhaps even more easily than, those who are virtuous. Fame belongs to the great, the outstanding, the exceptional, without regard to virtue or vice. Infamy is fame no less than good repute. The great scoundrel can be as famous as the great hero; there can be famous villains as well as famous saints. Existing in the reputation a person has regardless of his or her accomplishments, fame does not tarnish as honor does when it is unmerited.

We normally desire the esteem of our fellow human beings, but is not this wish for the esteem of others a desire for fame rather than for honor? Virtuous persons will not seek fame or be unhappy lacking it, for fame can be enjoyed by bad men as well as good. When it is enjoyed by good men without being sought by them, it is indistinguishable from honor for then it is deserved.

In a constitutional government, those who hold public office exercise more political power than other citizens who are not elected or appointed to administer government. But such power is vested constitutionally in the offices they hold, not in their persons. It is only personal power over others in all the worldly ventures in which they compete for power that is the object of wrong desire.

It is this wrong desire for the realization of which Machiavelli's *Prince* sets forth the rules, all of which can be summarized in the maxim of expediency. That maxim admonishes individuals who wrongly desire personal power over others to act virtuously if they can succeed by doing so, but if that cannot be done, then the maxim of expediency calls upon them to forsake virtue and to use, without scruple, foul means as well as fair in order to gain and to retain the power sought.

Machiavelli advises persons seeking power to be both lion and fox—to have both cunning and guile at their disposal as well as brute force—to have a reputation for virtue even when they abandon virtue as not expedient. "It is not necessary for a prince," he writes, to have the qualities of the virtuous person, but "it is very necessary to seem to have them"—to have the reputation for virtue; in other words, to be undeservedly famous. Machiavelli goes on as follows:

> I would even be bold to say that to possess [the qualities of virtue] and always to observe them is dangerous, but to appear to possess them is useful. . . . You must have a mind so disposed that when it is needful to be otherwise, you may be able to change to the opposite qualities. And it must be understood that a prince . . . cannot observe all those things which are considered good in men. . . . [You] must have a mind disposed to adapt itself according to the wind, and as the variations of fortune dictate . . . not deviate from what is good, if possible, but be able to do evil if constrained.

This maxim of expediency is often stated in the phrase "the end justifies the means." But those who appeal to that maxim usually misunderstand its true significance. A morally good end, such as the *totum bonum*, cannot be served by any means that are not themselves morally good—means that ought to be sought by right desires in the pursuit of happiness. But good means do not need justification. It is only immoral means, wrongly desired, that need justification; and they can only be justified when they are judged to be expedient for the purpose of succeeding in the achievement of a morally wrong end—personal power over others, to be gained and retained by the unscrupulous recourse to unjust means.

Fame and power are thus linked together as objects of wrong desire. The reputation for virtue when that is a means to be sought by persons seeking personal power in the rat race of worldly ventures is the fame that is wrongly desired as expedient for success in striving for an objective that is itself wrongly desired as an end.

CHAPTER 4

RIGHT DESIRES

The Totum Bonum and Its Constituents

1

THE DISCUSSION IN CHAPTER 2 of happiness as the *totum bonum* was insufficient for our treatment here of right desires. As we saw in Chapter 3, the variety of wrong desires stem from substituting for the *totum bonum*, one or another partial good, real or merely apparent, and elevating it to the position of the complete good and ultimate goal of striving.

From this fact arises the striking difference between wrong and right desires. There are many alternative and exclusive wrong desires, each aiming at a different wrong end. But although right desires are also many, there is a conjunction of them because they all aim at the same right end—the *totum bonum* or complete good.

Furthermore, all right desires aim at real goods or at apparent goods that are innocuous and so permissible. In contrast, the objects of wrong desires are apparent goods that are not innocuous (such as fame or power) or they are real goods (such as pleasure and money) which, as means to happiness, are partial goods, not the complete good.

One group of wrongly motivated individuals may be exclusively pleasure-seeking; another group, exclusively money-mad; another, power-hungry, and so on. They represent the variety of bad moral characters to be found in society. They often come into conflict with one another in pursuit of their alternative goals.

In sharp contrast, persons motivated by right desire, while differing in minor traits, are all of the same moral character. Moral virtue is the same in all of them. It is only with respect to the moral vices that we find the variety alluded to above. In the sphere of thought the relation between truth and error is a one-many relation: for every basic truth there is a multiplicity of errors. The relation of moral virtue to the many vices is the same.

When we define moral virtue as the habit of right desire, we must not overlook its complexity. Moral virtue has many aspects and involves many right desires. In the first place, moral virtue is concerned with both the one right end and all the means thereto. The one right end is the object of the will's habitually virtuous intention; the right means are the objects of the will's virtuous acts of choice. In the second place, the multiplicity of right desires arises from the multiplicity of real goods that ought to be sought as means to happiness.

Among this multiplicity of means to happiness, the basic distinction to be made is between (a) means that are operative, functioning as causal factors in the pursuit of happiness, and (b) means that are constitutive, functioning as component partial goods in the whole good that is the *totum bonum*.

Moral virtue is itself one of the two operative means to happiness. Without it, no one can effectively pursue happiness. But though it is necessary, it is not sufficient for the pursuit of happiness. Good fortune is also required as the other necessary but not sufficient condition, conferring on individuals real goods that they cannot attain entirely by their own power of free choice. They may rightly desire such goods, but their possession of them depends partly on external circumstances, either the beneficence of good luck or the benefactions of organized society under a just government that attempts to secure for its members the real goods they need, to which they have a natural right, but which they cannot attain entirely by their own power of choice.

Some of these circumstantially dependent goods are partly goods of chance and partly goods of choice; others are entirely goods of chance, not within the power of virtuous individuals to attain nor within the power of a just government to secure and bestow. The only real good that is entirely a good of choice is moral virtue itself as the operative means to happiness.

Since the multiplicity of real goods derives from the multiplicity of needs inherent in human nature, it should be possible to give an exhaustive enumeration of them. The following inventory may not be exhaustive, but I think it is a fairly close approximation.

First come the bodily needs that we have in common with other animals: the need for food, drink, sleep, and protection from the inclemencies of the environment, in the form of shelter or clothing.

Then there are a number of bodily needs—for health and for pleasure. If wealth is named as a real good to be sought, it covers all the commodities needed to sustain life and health decently—all the necessities and amenities of a decent human livelihood.

In addition, human beings need to associate with one another for they are by nature social animals. Human associations, domestic and civil, are among the real goods to be sought. With regard to both, and especially with regard to the larger community, civil peace is to be sought. Still to be added among the distinctively human goods needed are freedom or liberty, loves or friendships, the dignity of honor or the deserved respect of others with whom one is associated, and finally knowledge in all its forms, especially understanding and wisdom.

The foregoing inventory names only the real goods that are constitutive components of happiness as the *totum bonum*. I have not named the two operative means, the two causal factors involved in its pursuit—moral virtue and good fortune. Only one of these is a real good that we are morally obliged to seek as an object of right desire. Good fortune cannot be sought; it is not an object of right desire. We may wish for it or pray for it, but we cannot choose between seeking it or not doing so.

Among these real goods, some are merely means to others and some are ends as well as means, desired for their own sake as well as means to happiness. Happiness itself, though an object of right desire, should not be included in the inventory of real goods, for it is not one good among others, or even the highest of the real goods, the *summum bonum*. When it is identified with the *totum bonum*, it is not *a* good to be sought as a means or even as *an* end but *the* good to be sought as *the ultimate end*, sought for its own sake and sought as the complete good that leaves nothing more to be desired.

The pursuit of happiness on earth is seldom, if ever, completely effective, because life on earth is beset by many misfortunes, many of them serious, and because few human beings, if any, are completely or perfectly virtuous. Those who do achieve some measure of happiness achieve it in varying degrees because their lives are attended by strokes of good fortune and because they manage to be reasonably, if not perfectly, virtuous.

---- 2 ----

One problem about the pursuit of happiness remains to be discussed before we turn to the consideration of specific right desires that deserve special examination.

The one categorical obligation, which is the only self-evident principle in moral philosophy, appears to be self-regarding. As stated earlier, it is that each of us ought to seek everything that is really good for us and nothing else, though we may also be permitted to seek apparent goods that are innocuous.

Is this principle entirely self-regarding? Beyond our own individual happiness, have we no moral obligation to seek the happiness of others, either all other human beings on earth, or at least all the fellow human beings who are members of the same society, persons with whom we are associated and with whom we live together?

Moreover, are we sometimes not morally obliged to subordinate the pursuit of our own happiness to acting for the happiness of others, and even to sacrifice some of the real goods that we rightly desire for ourselves in order to serve better the pursuit of happiness by others?

Undoubtedly, there are some completely selfish individuals who would answer these questions with negative responses and would do so without apologies or shame. But my general sense of the matter is that most human beings are both selfish and altruistic. They would either unhesitatingly affirm our moral obligation to serve the pursuit of happiness by others, or they would at least be seriously troubled by a moral philosophy that appeared to be entirely self-regarding, as a moral philosophy appears to be if it is based on the undeniable moral obligation of each individual to seek all the real goods he or she needs in the pursuit of his or her own happiness.

On the face of it, there is the appearance of selfishness in the statement of our moral obligation as one that enjoins each of us to seek what is really good for us. That seems to be confirmed by the fact that there is no correspondingly undeniable truth in the statement that each of us ought to seek the happiness of others.

If each of us has that moral obligation in addition to the moral obligation to seek our own happiness, so that the pursuit of happiness is both altruistic and selfish, what makes the maxim that calls for altruism prescriptively true, since it is clearly not undeniable or self-evident?[1]

3

The solution of the problem lies in the fact that moral virtue is both self-regarding and other-regarding in its different aspects. To flesh this solution out in all its details, we must now consider five points that explain why selfishness and altruism, far from being antagonistic opposites, are inseparable in the virtuous person.

1. We must first distinguish between individual and common goods. Being the same for all human beings, responsive

1. This is a problem to which Aristotle alone has a satisfactory solution. It is a problem that two of the greatest moral philosophers in modern times— Immanuel Kant and John Stuart Mill—signally fail to solve. I will point out their deficiencies in Chapter 5.

to needs inherent in their specific human nature, real goods are common. They do not differ from individual to individual, as do the innocuous apparent goods that are different for different individuals. The latter being objects only of permissible desires, we are not morally obliged to seek these apparent goods—the objects of our individually different wants, not of our common human needs.

Hence if we are ever called upon to defer or abandon our striving for these individual goods in order to serve the pursuit of happiness by others, that in no way defeats or frustrates the pursuit of our own happiness. It does not challenge the truth of the statement that each of us ought to seek what is really good for us and nothing else. There is no "ought" attached to the wanting of merely apparent goods that each of us may permissibly desire.

2. There is a second meaning of the term "common good." The real goods needed by all human beings are common in the sense of being the same objects of right desire for all human beings. This first sense can be designated by the Latin phrase *bonum commune hominis*. But there is a good that is common in the sense that all who live in the same society participate in it as a means that serves the pursuit of happiness by each. This second sense can be designated by *bonum commune communitatis*.

It is the general welfare, the public good, of the civil community as a whole. It consists in all the conditions that a civil society, justly governed, provides for its citizens to aid the pursuit by each of his or her own happiness. These conditions are real goods that are not wholly within the power of each person to secure for himself or herself.[2]

3. The third point follows closely on the second. Our

---

2. See Note 4 in Appendix I.

natural needs are not only the basis for distinguishing between real and merely apparent goods. They are also the basis from which all our natural—our human and unalienable—rights are derived. Precisely because many or most of these real goods are not entirely within our power to attain for ourselves, we have a right to any of them that it is within the power of a just government to secure for us. A government is just only to the extent that it secures all the rights of its citizens, thereby aiding them in the pursuit by each of his or her own happiness by helping them to attain the real goods they need and rightly desire, but cannot attain entirely by their own power.

4. Justice on the part of each individual is one of the four cardinal aspects of moral virtue. It is the other-regarding aspect of moral virtue, in contrast to the self-regarding aspects that are called temperance and courage or fortitude. What does justice require each of us to do with regard to the pursuit of happiness by others? Two things, one negative, the other positive.

The negative aspect of justice is the obligation *not* to injure others by impeding or frustrating their pursuit of happiness by transgressing or violating their natural rights and thus interfering with their attainment of real goods they need. The positive aspect of justice is the obligation to act for the common good of the community in which we and others live and in which we together participate.

We are not morally obliged positively to act *directly* for the happiness of others. Only generous acts of love are altruistically benevolent. Aristotle summed this up in a single sentence when he said that if all human beings were friends, loving one another, there would be no need for justice. In our *direct* relation to others, our moral obligation to others is negative: not to injure them. It is only in our *indirect* relation to others, through acting for the public common good or general welfare, in which others as well as we ourselves participate, that we are obliged to act positively.[3]

It should be obvious that the other two aspects of moral virtue—temperance and courage or fortitude—are entirely self-regarding. Temperance is moderation in our desire for goods that are limited goods. It calls upon us to defer the gratification of immediate desires for the sake of living a good life as a whole. Courage or fortitude enjoins us to take and suffer certain immediate pains for the sake of living a good life as a whole. In the absence of these two aspects of moral virtue, we cannot effectively pursue happiness, which consists in trying to make a life that is morally good and enriched by the cumulative possession of all real goods.

There is a fourth cardinal aspect of moral virtue, in addition to the three so far named. It is prudence or practical wisdom, which consists in the choice of the right means for the right end—the *totum bonum*. As temperance and courage or fortitude habitually dispose us to act always for the right end (a good life as a whole), so prudence habitually disposes us to choose the right means for that purpose.

If an individual chooses effective means for the wrong end, as the burglar does who breaks into a house in a way that avoids detection and apprehension, he should not be called prudent, but only smart or clever. Such cleverness is a counterfeit of prudence. So, too, there is a counterfeit of temperance in the businessman who moderates his desire for immediate pleasures but only for the sake of increasing his wealth; a counterfeit of fortitude in the professional athlete who takes pain in perfecting his performance but only for the fame he may thereby gain.

3. See Notes 5, 6, and 7 in Appendix I.

5. The point just made about prudence and its counterfeit, as well as the counterfeits of temperance and courage, helps us to understand the final and crucial point that explains why moral virtue is inseparably self-regarding and other-regarding.

Let me explain first the two ways in which things are separable and inseparable. They can be separated existentially or be inseparable existentially; and they can be separated analytically or be inseparable analytically. For example, butter on one plate and toast on another are existentially separate. However, when the hot toast is buttered, the toast and the butter are existentially inseparable, even though we can analytically—by perception and thought—distinguish between the taste of the butter on the toast and the taste of the buttered toast.

The full solution of the problem with which we are here concerned is a doctrine that is uniquely Aristotelian, not even shared by his disciple Thomas Aquinas. It is the doctrine of the unity of virtue—the doctrine that the cardinal virtues named above are not four existentially separate virtues, any one of which is capable of existing in the absence of the others, but only four analytically separate aspects of moral virtue.

This means that a man cannot be genuinely prudent without also being at the same time genuinely temperate, courageous, and just. The counterfeits of these aspects of virtue, as we have seen, can exist in separation, but no one can be genuinely prudent without also being genuinely temperate, courageous, and just; and, if that is the case, no one can be temperate and courageous without being just, or just without being temperate and courageous.

Why is this so? The answer is that moral virtue, in its aspects of temperance, fortitude, and justice, is the habitual disposition to aim at the *totum bonum* as the right end, and moral virtue in its aspect of prudence chooses the right means to that end.

Another way of saying this is that the choice of the means, to be the right choice, must be made for the right reason (i.e., the right end) and striving for the right end must involve the right choice of means required for achieving it. The unity of moral virtue (i.e., the existential inseparability of its four cardinal aspects) derives from its being at once habitually disposed to desire the right end and to choose means for that end, which is the only right reason for choosing them.

Since I cannot effectively pursue my own happiness as the *totum bonum* unless I am temperate and courageous, and since I cannot be temperate and courageous without being just, my self-regarding obligations and right desires are inseparable from my other-regarding obligations and right desires.

The Golden Rule, so often repeated in so many different phrasings (including the phrasing of Kant's categorical imperative) is a vacuous maxim without this understanding of the unity of moral virtue. Unless I know what is really good for me, I cannot know what is really good for every other human being—goods they need to which they have a natural right that I, in justice, must respect. In other words, without knowing what I would have them do unto me (because I know the real goods to which I have a natural right), I cannot know what I should do unto them reciprocally.

The person who aims at the wrong end will not be motivated by other-regarding considerations. Striving for the wrong goal in life, misplacing his happiness in the endless accumulation of money, the man without moral virtue may exhibit counterfeits of temperance and courage, and even prudence in his choice of means. But in the pursuit of the wrong end, he will be unscrupulously expedient in choosing whatever works best, even if that involves his being unjust to others.

Only the wrong end can justify such expediency in the choice of means. Only good means can serve the pursuit of the right end, and so here the means do not need justification. The maxim about the end justifying the means applies only to the unscrupulous expediency required for the pursuit of wrong ends.

Those who seek the same wrong end (such as the endless accumulation of money) or persons who seek different wrong ends (such as maximizing pleasure or power) will be competitive in their pursuit of happiness, come into conflict, and act unjustly toward others. It is only for persons who are morally virtuous, striving for the same end, that the pursuit of happiness is cooperative rather than competitive.

—— 4 ——

That freedom or liberty—the words are synonymous—is a real good and ought to be desired as an indispensable component of the *totum bonum* needs no argument. But freedom can be wrongly desired as well as rightly desired; and, in addition, there are forms of freedom that cannot be objects of desire at all.

Let us, first of all, eliminate the forms or modes of freedom that cannot be objects of desire. In its two-volume study of the idea of freedom, the Institute for Philosophical Research distinguished three main types of freedom by two identifying criteria.[4]

4. See *The Idea of Freedom*, Volume I (1958) and Volume II (1961), especially Volume I, pp. 167–620.

One criterion was the way in which individuals possessed the freedom: either by nature, or by acquisition, or by circumstances. Free will, or freedom of choice, is either a natural freedom, with which all human beings are endowed, or it does not exist at all. One may wish that the facts of human nature affirmed the existence of such freedom, but if human beings have freedom of choice by natural endowment, it is not an object of desire.[5]

The second criterion for distinguishing the three forms of freedom is the characterization of them when they are possessed. In what do they consist? For example, freedom of choice, which we identified as a natural endowment, consists in being able always to choose otherwise, no matter how, or on any occasion, we actually do choose. We have described it as the freedom of self-determination.

Another of the main forms of freedom is one that some human beings acquire and others do not. Acquired freedom consists in being able to will as one ought. We therefore described it as a freedom of self-perfection, the freedom possessed by the morally virtuous who have acquired the habit of conforming their will to the mandates of morality and to the just prescriptions of the civil law.

Forms of liberty are often described negatively as well as positively: they are not only freedoms that consist in having certain abilities to act in certain ways, but they are also freedoms from certain conditions. Thus, the freedom of self-determination is freedom from causal determination by antecedent conditions in one's makeup and in one's life; and

---

5. The word "wish" signifies a hope rather than a desire, because the object wished for is something beyond the power of the individual's own effort to obtain. All goods of fortune, as well as all gifts of love, are objects of hope that we wish for, but do not desire in the sense that desire motivates executive action on our part. Wishes are not effectual motivations.

the acquired freedom of self-perfection is freedom from the passions that often impel one to act contrary to the dictates of virtue. The fourth book of Spinoza's *Ethics* is entitled "Of the passions or of human bondage." Boethius in prison exults in the possession of such freedom, which has also been called moral liberty.

If human beings do not in fact naturally possess the freedom of self-determination, neither can they enjoy the freedom of self-perfection. Those who are not always free to choose cannot have the freedom to will as they ought. The nonexistence of the first form of freedom makes the second form of freedom also nonexistent; and even if the first form of freedom does exist, other factors may lead to the denial of existence to the second form of freedom.

If there are no objectively true oughts, if there is no distinction between right and wrong desires, the notion of moral virtue becomes devoid of sense. Hence, there is no moral liberty either, no freedom of self-perfection. In any case, this second form of freedom, even if it can be correctly affirmed to exist, is desirable only in the sense that individuals can freely choose to be or not to be morally virtuous. So considered, it is moral virtue that is rightly desired as an operative or functional means in the pursuit of happiness. The freedom of self-perfection is desirable only as a consequence of desiring to be morally virtuous.

We come now to the third of the three main forms of liberty—the freedom that individuals enjoy under favorable circumstances and of which they are deprived by the unfavorable circumstances that surround their lives and actions. We characterized such circumstantial freedom as a freedom of self-realization, possessed by individuals who are free from the coercion or duress that prevents them from being able to act as they please, and of being able to execute the free choices they make. The economist R. H. Tawney adds another negative note when he says that the poor man is not free to dine at the Ritz because his circumstances are such that he *lacks* the enabling means to do so.

It is such circumstantial freedom that Thomas Jefferson had in mind when, among unalienable natural rights, he listed liberty. We either have or do not have the freedom of self-determination as a natural endowment, but we do not have a natural right to it. We either have the freedom of self-perfection as something we acquire by becoming morally virtuous, but we do not have a natural right to it. We cannot be deprived of it by the actions of others or by the laws of the society in which we live. When we claim the circumstantial freedom of self-realization—the liberty to do as we please, freedom from externally imposed impediments to freedom of action—we are speaking of a freedom to which a natural human right can be claimed because it is indispensable to the pursuit of happiness. Without it our freedom of choice would be nugatory.

It is this third form of freedom that is then an object of right desire for which individuals have appealed and fought throughout human history. As an object of right desire, it is one among the real goods that are components of the *totum bonum*, indispensable to living a good human life. But it is, like wealth, a real good that is not entirely within the individual's power to achieve by his own efforts. Only a good society, one justly governed, eliminating all forms of human slavery and subjection, confers upon its members this desirable circumstantial freedom of self-realization.

Though this third form of freedom is desirable and can be rightly desired, it is also an object that can be wrongly desired. How so? By being desired without any limitation whatsoever. Those who call themselves libertarians are prone to the error of thinking that one should be free to do anything one pleases. The right desire for liberty of action in society is not for unconstrained autonomy, but for limited liberty.

How much liberty of action is rightly desired? The answer is that individuals ought to desire the liberty to do as they please only if they can exercise that freedom without injuring others and without depriving others of their freedom to do as they please. Human beings should have no more freedom than they can use justly in obedience to just laws, civil or moral, and in relation to the good of other human beings. Only when it is thus limited is the circumstantial freedom of self-realization rightly desired.

When those who are morally virtuous obey just laws, especially laws that prohibit them from injuring others, they are doing as they please. The freedom of self-realization is not freedom from law. The sphere of liberty does not increase with the diminution of the sphere of legal regulation. If there were no justly enacted laws, which restrained individuals from injuring others, liberty would be diminished. Criminals who successfully disobey just laws enjoy license, not liberty.

The circumstantial freedom of self-realization includes political liberty as well as freedom of action. Man is by nature a political animal whose self-realization consists not only in being able to do as he or she pleases but also in being governed with his or her own consent and with a voice in his or her own government.

This is the reason why constitutional democracy is the only perfectly just form of government. Through its constitutional enactment of universal suffrage, it confers citizenship, and with it political liberty, on all human beings, with the just exception of infants (below the age of consent), of the mentally incompetent in asylums, and of incarcerated felonious criminals.

Unlike the freedom to do as one pleases, which is an object of right desire only when it is desired as a limited freedom, political liberty is *always* an object of right desire and, as so desired, it is desired *without* any limitation.

There is one further difference between political liberty and freedom of action in society as objects of right desire.

Only morally virtuous individuals rightly desire freedom of action, for only they desire it as a limited freedom; but political liberty is an object of right desire for individuals whether or not they are morally virtuous. The freedom of self-realization presupposes the freedom of self-perfection when the freedom to do as one pleases is an object of right desire, but not when it is political liberty.

Both freedom of action in society and political liberty as objects of right desire are also real goods needed for the pursuit of happiness, to which all human beings have an unalienable natural right. Their possession of this right does not depend on their being or not being morally virtuous individuals, nor does that fact make freedom of action always an object of right desire, as it does in the case of political liberty.

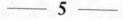

5

As in the case of pleasure, so also in the case of love, a psychological understanding must precede the consideration of the moral problems involved. To deal with love as an object of right desire, we must first clarify the relation of love to desire; and, in addition, we must call attention to the prevalent misuse of the word "love" in everyday speech.

The word "love" is generally misused as if it were a synonym of "desire." When children, and their elders as well, say that they love pleasant things to eat or drink, or that they love to do this or that, they think they are saying no more than that they like something, that it pleases them, or that they want it. This misuse of the word is corrected, though it probably will never be prevented, by a better understanding of the relation between love and desire than most people have.

The most basic psychological distinction in the sphere of our mental acts and in our overt behavior is made by the line that divides the cognitive from the appetitive. Our desires and emotions or passions belong on the appetitive side of that line; our acts of knowing, understanding, and thinking, on the cognitive side.

In the appetitive sphere, the most fundamental distinction is between acquisitive and benevolent desire. It is the latter to which the word "love," properly used, should be attached.

The prime characteristic of the appetitive is its tendency or impulse to act in a certain way toward the object of appetite, whatever that may be. This tendency or impulse is usually, but not always, accompanied by feelings or sentiments, sometimes involving almost overpowering bodily turmoil, as in the case of fear and anger, and sometimes quite mild affections, as in the case of some bodily pleasures and pains.

Putting aside the emotional or feeling aspect of our appetites, let us consider here only the tendencies or impulses to action that are involved in such things as desiring—wanting, needing, and loving.

Hunger and thirst are the most obvious examples of acquisitive desire experienced by everyone at one time or another. We often eat without being hungry and drink without being thirsty. But when we are famished or parched, we experience a strong desire or impulse to go and get something edible or drinkable. That tendency or impulse is acquisitive desire in its most obvious manifestation.

In every instance of acquisitive desire we are impelled to seek something for ourselves—to get it, lay hold of it, consume it, appropriate or possess it in some way. All acquisitive desires are selfish in the sense that they are self-seeking impulses, desires that, when satisfied, leave us momentarily contented.

When we experience such acquisitive desires and are impelled by them to such self-satisfying actions, we say, "I want this" or "I need it." The difference between wanting and needing has already been made clear.

But not all our desires or appetitive impulses are acquisitive and self-seeking. We sometimes, even often, have desires and consequent impulses to do something for the benefit of another. We are impelled to give to another instead of getting something for ourselves.

Just as the words "want" and "need," properly used, name all the forms of acquisitive desire, so the word "love," properly used, should be reserved for all forms of benevolent desire—and for the impulse to give rather than to get. As acquisitive desires and getting represent the selfish aspect of our lives, so benevolent desires and giving represent the altruistic aspect.

We are selfish when we are exclusively or predominantly concerned with the good for ourselves. We are altruistic when we are exclusively or predominantly concerned with the good of others. Our selfish impulses are all for our own benefit. Our altruistic impulses are all for the benefit of others. To act benevolently is to confer benefits upon others.

If people generally misuse the words "need" and "want," saying they need when they mean they want, it is even more generally the case that all of us misuse the word "love." Children, and not only children, say they love ice cream, or that they would love to have a sailboat or a sports car. Such things are not loved; no benevolent desire or impulse is involved. We also say we love our freedom, which is something we certainly need but do not love. Only when we say that we love our friends, our spouses, or our children, and perhaps even our country, is the word "love" being used properly.

Even then, when we use the word to express our feelings about or impulses toward another person, it is not always the case that we are properly using the word "love." For example, when young children say they love their parents, they do not mean that they have any benevolent impulses toward them. On the contrary, they do need their parents for a variety of the goods they acquisitively desire and that they want their parents to get for them and give to them. Parents, on the other hand, who are unselfishly concerned with the good of their children and are impelled to confer upon them all the benefits within their power to bestow, truly love their children.

In the sphere of our adolescent and adult relationships, we often say that we love other persons when, in fact, we need them for some self-satisfaction or want them for some selfish purpose. Not present at all is any benevolent impulse exclusively or predominantly concerned with the good of the other.

There are four things that one person can say to another: "I want you"; "I need you"; I like you"; and "I love you." If one wants another only for some self-satisfaction, usually in the form of sensual pleasure, that wrong desire takes the form of lust rather than love. If one needs another for some selfish purpose, such as acquiring wealth, the desire is still acquisitive rather than benevolent. Only when loving another is rooted in liking or admiring that other—and when our liking of what we find good in that person impels us to do what we can to benefit him or her—is it correct to say that we love that person. We can, of course, like persons that we do not love; but with one important exception, to be noted presently, we cannot love persons (in the sense of having benevolent impulses toward them) without first liking them, which consists in admiring what is good about them.

We have only one word in English for "love," where speakers of ancient Greek and Latin had three words. The three Greek words were *eros*, *philia*, and *agape*. The three Latin words were *amor*, *amicitia*, and *caritas*. But in addition to the word "love" in English, we also have such words as "friendship" and "charity," and such phrases as "erotic love" and "sexual love."

The Greeks used the word *eros* and the Romans used the word *amor* for the kind of love we call erotic, amorous, or sexual. Such love may involve sexual pleasure. Nevertheless, it is love rather than sexual lust or unbridled sexuality if, in addition to the need or want involved, there is also some impulse to give pleasure to the persons thus loved and not merely to use them for our own selfish pleasure.

When no sexual desire and impulse is involved in our relation to another person that we say we love, we have the form of friendship that the Greeks called *philia* and the Romans *amicitia*. We like others for the virtues in them that we admire; and because we admire or like them, we love them in the sense of wishing to act for their good and to enhance it by whatever benefits we can confer upon them.

This does not exclude obtaining self-satisfaction from such love. It may not be totally altruistic. A friend whom one loves in this way is an alter ego. We love him or her as we love ourselves. We feel one with them. Conjugal love, or the friendship of spouses, persists after sexual desires have weakened, withered, and disappeared.

Finally, the third kind of love, which the Greeks called *agape* and the Romans *caritas*, we sometimes refer to as "charitable love," and sometimes as "divine love," or the love of God and of human beings, ourselves and others, as creatures of God. Such love is totally unselfish, totally altruistic. We bestow such love even on persons we do not admire and, therefore, do not like. It is giving without any getting. It is the love that impels one human being to lay down his life for another.

It is not a misunderstanding of love or a misuse of the word to associate love with sexual desire. Erotic or sexual love can truly be love if it is not selfishly sexual or lustful.

But only one who understands the existence of love in a world totally devoid of sex—one who uses the word "love" to signify the benevolent impulses we have toward others whom we like and admire and call our friends—can claim to understand the meaning of love as distinguished from the purely acquisitive desires we have when we need or want things or persons for our own sake and for self-satisfaction.

However, when we say that we love the truth, or when we interpret the word "philosophy" etymologically as signifying the love of wisdom, we are departing from the understanding of love as benevolent desire.[6]

---

6. In contrast to "philosophy," the word "philanthropy," etymologically interpreted, correctly signifies benevolence toward humankind, and accordingly all philanthropic institutions and activities engaged in charitable bequests are motivated by a love of mankind.

We may admire truth or wisdom; we may even pursue the truth or seek wisdom as objects of right desire; but we are not impelled to act benevolently toward them. Our impulse to make the truth available to mankind or to increase its store of wisdom may be a benevolent concomitant of our great admiration for truth and wisdom, but that benevolence flows from our love of humanity, not from our love or truth or wisdom.

—— 6 ——

In the light of this psychological analysis and these terminological clarifications, what can we say about love as an object of right desire?

Is loving other human beings and being loved by them a component of the *totum bonum*, something we need in order to live well and pursue happiness? Everything else being equal, does the person who has moral virtue and is blessed by good fortune lead a better life than another person, if the former's life is enriched by friendships that involved requited love while the latter's life is deprived both of loving others and being loved by them?

I have introduced the word "friendship" for that human relationship which involves love. Aristotle writes of lower forms of friendship, motivated not by love, but by pleasure or utility, calling the highest form of friendship one that stems from the admiration a virtuous person has for another person of similar virtue that impels each of the two persons to act benevolently toward the other. It is only about this highest form of friendship that we are asking whether it is an indispensable constituent of the *totum bonum*. If our answer is affirmative, we are then affirming that love is an object of right desire.

The fact that we are by nature social animals and need to live in the company of our fellow human beings underlies our need for love, over and above our need to live in society, not in solitude. Living in society is not enough. We do not share our lives with all of our compatriots; nor do we like or admire all of them.

Christ's two precepts of charity command Christians to love all their fellow human beings whether they like them or not; but charity, as we have seen, is divine or supernatural love and requires the grace of God.

On the purely natural plane, we are under a moral obligation to act justly toward everyone, yet that does not mean that we must act benevolently toward them, but only that, in justly respecting their human rights, we must not injure them or hinder their pursuit of happiness. The generosity of love is positive and exceeds the negative obligations of justice. As we have already seen, that is why Aristotle tells us that if all human beings were friends, there would be no need for justice between them.

The desire to share one's life with others, and to live one's days in their company, is rooted in our social nature, but it is much more specific than our natural need to live socially rather than in solitude. It stems from the love we bear those whom we call our friends. It stems also from the love we wish them to bestow upon us. To live in society but without close friends is almost as contrary to man's nature as to live in complete solitude.

The good man, Aristotle writes, needs other similarly good men to do well by, going on to say, "That is why the question is asked whether we need friends more in prosperity than in adversity . . . for it is better to spend one's days with friends and good men than with strangers or any chance persons," and concluding with the statement that "a virtuous friend seems to be naturally desirable for a virtuous man. . . . The man who is to be happy will therefore need virtuous friends."[7]

7

It is of the utmost importance to observe a difference that often goes unnoticed. This failure accounts for the fact that that term *summum bonum* (literally, the highest good), in much of moral philosophy, has taken on the significance that should be reserved for the *totum bonum* (literally, the whole or complete good), as if the highest good were the final end of human striving.

The difference between these two goods is plainly noted in the first book of Aristotle's *Ethics*, when he says of happiness that it is the final end, the complete good which, unlike all the partial goods, leaves nothing more to be desired. In other words, *the* good is not one good among others, whereas every other good, each properly referred to as *a* good, is just one good among many. Hence the possession of any partial good leaves other goods to be desired, and therefore is not to be identified as the final end.

Many discourses on ethical or moral matters concentrate on the *summum bonum* and ignore the *totum bonum*. For them the *summum bonum* stands for the supreme good, the ideal perfection toward which we should strive, and regard ourselves as happy when we attain it to any degree.

7. See *Nicomachean Ethics*, Book IX, Chapter 9; see also Book VIII, Chapters 1–4.

Moral virtue is often denominated as the *summum bonum*, the supreme good, although it is only one of the two operative or functional means in the pursuit of happiness, the other being the blessings of good fortune. Those who make the mistake of wrongly desiring pleasure, money or wealth, fame and power, as if these partial goals were the goals of human striving, regard these real or apparent goods as if one or another of them were the supreme good.

At the beginning of this chapter, readers found an inventory of the partial goods that are components of the complete good, either constituents of it or functional means to its attainment in a complete life. They were not only enumerated there, but they were put in an order of inferior or superior goods, some of them being good merely as means and others good as ends in themselves while at the same time they are means to happiness, which is the only end that is not also a means.

The question we must now consider is whether, among all these partial goods, there is one that is the supreme good—the *summum bonum*. If there is such a good, then it must also be the prime object of right desire, of greater value than all the other objects of right desire, to the attainment of which all other partial goods should be subordinated. In answering this question, we should never forget that the attainment of this one supreme good does not constitute happiness or a morally good life. Though it is the supreme good, the attainment of it leaves other goods to be rightly desired, all of which together in a complete life, conducted virtuously and blessed by good fortune, make that life a happy one.

The foregoing paragraph briefly summarizes the message of Book I of the *Nicomachean Ethics*, the central vision of which is that happiness is the *totum bonum*—the complete good and not one good among others. Among the partial goods that constitute happiness as its components, the highest or supreme partial good is the *summum bonum*. This is never to be confused with the *totum bonum*, since it is only one of its component elements.

A problem about the *summum bonum* remains for us to consider. It focuses on Aristotle's use of the word *theoría* in Book X, Chapters 7 and 8. He uses that word in describing the *summum bonum* while at the same time reiterating his teaching in Book I about the *totum bonum*. The word *theoría* had a wide range of meanings in Greek. It is usually rendered in English by translators of Aristotle's *Ethics* by the word "contemplation," which is also richly ambiguous.

The Greek word *theoría*, usually translated as "contemplation," was used for being a spectator at games or at the theater; for viewing, beholding, or inspecting; for consideration, and for thinking when that is done for its own sake rather than for the sake of the action to which thinking may lead. In Book VI, where Aristotle classifies and discusses the intellectual virtues: two of them, art and prudence, are virtues of the practical intellect, concerned with making and doing; and three of them are virtues of the theoretical or speculative intellect, understanding, science, and wisdom. English translations of Book VI do not call any of the latter three "contemplative virtues."

When we come to the English words "contemplation" and "contemplative," the difficulty increases, partly because in Christian theology, the word "contemplation" is used for the religious activity of prayer. When Aquinas in the *Summa Theologica* treats the two modes of the monastic life, he calls one "active" and the other "contemplative," the latter being life in those religious orders dedicated exclusively to prayer. In addition, the word "contemplation" is used in

Christian theology for the beatific vision—the intuitive beholding of God by souls in the heavenly communion of saints. On earth, an analogous human experience is the aesthetic experience—the intuitive beholding of a work of art. In such experience, the intellect is not involved in the process of discursive thought. Such experience is, therefore, quite different from the theoretical activity of the mind when it is involved in thought for the sake of understanding, coming to have scientific or philosophical knowledge, and attaining some modicum of wisdom.

Not all the activity of the intellect is discursive and ratiocinative. The understanding of principles is not; and when, after research and reasoning, we arrive at true conclusions, beholding those truths is an intuitive, not a discursive, act of the intellect. After its efforts, our mind comes to rest in the truths we have learned and we take delight in beholding them. It is for this restful delight that Aristotle uses the word *theoría*, and it is in this sense that we may be said to engage in intellectual contemplation.

Our ordinary use of the word "contemplate" tends in the opposite direction to carry the connotation of discursive thinking. When one person says to another, "Did you consider doing that?" the reply is likely to be "No, I did not contemplate it" or "I did not think about doing it." This usage of the word in ordinary English speech is a far cry from the sense in which most English translations of Book X suggest that the *summum bonum*, the supreme good in the pattern of a happy life, is engagement by philosophers in the contemplation of truth, a human activity that, in Aristotle's antique theology, is most akin to the activity of the divine intellect.

Even if we dismiss this ancient view and use the word "contemplation" for an intuitive act of the mind, we are left with the problem of defining the *summum bonum* in such a way that it is accessible to all members of the human species, at least all who are not pathologically defective. Only a few human beings engage for the most part in philosophical thought, in the ratiocinative pursuit of and terminal contemplation of philosophical truth.

The most fundamental principle in moral philosophy must guide us here; namely, that whatever is the final end, rightly sought, must be a final end that is appropriate, in varying degrees of attainment, for all members of the human species, not just a very few.

Most human beings engage mainly in what Aristotle calls the active or political life, in contrast to the life of philosophical thought, even if it is true that philosophy is everybody's business, and that all men, in varying degrees, should philosophize. Here we must pay attention to Aristotle's point that the life of thought or the speculative life is superior to the life of action or the practical life because it is less dependent on external and contingent circumstances.

Before I offer my own solution of the problem concerning the *summum bonum*, I should say that my twentieth-century standpoint is clearly different from Aristotle's standpoint in Greek antiquity. Mine is democratic; his, aristocratic. Mine affirms the essential quality of all human beings, none of whom is more or less human than another, though in possessing the species-specific properties of human nature, they are also unequal in the degree to which they possess them. Aristotle appears to deny this in his views about human beings who are by nature intended for slavery and in his views about female inferiority.

What can we find in Book X, Chapters 7 and 8, that helps us to translate it into modern and democratic terms? In these two chapters, Aristotle introduces the triad of (1) play or amusement, (2) work or toil, and (3) leisure; and of these three human activities, only leisure activities are pursued for their own sake. Play or amusement is recreational and for the sake of work, and work is for the sake of leisure.

With this in mind, I am led to the insight that the highest good in a morally good life—the *summum bonum* in the *totum bonum*—is engagement in the pursuits of leisure in whatever time is free from engagement in all the other parts of a human life—sleep, play, and work or toil.[8] The pursuits of leisure are, for the most part, activities by which human beings learn and grow and thereby acquire one or more of the intellectual virtues.

The intellectual virtues of art, knowledge, understanding, and wisdom are the *summum bonum* that should be rightly desired and, in varying degrees, attainable by all human beings, just as moral virtue is attainable by all. Intellectual virtue and moral virtue play different roles in relation to the pursuit of happiness. Moral virtue, along with the blessings of good fortune, is an operative means to happiness, while intellectual virtue, of all the partial goods that constitute happiness, is the highest good—the *summum bonum* in the *totum bonum*.

If we use the word "work" for all economic activity aimed at obtaining the necessities, comforts, and conveniences of life, and the word "leisure" for all the creative activities of the intellect, the ensuing generalization is that engagement in leisure pursuits is the *summum bonum*.

To say that leisuring is the supreme good as an object of right desire is tantamount to saying that learning is the *sum-*

---

8. See *A Vision of the Future* (1984), Chapter 2, for a fuller discussion of work, play, and leisure among the parts of human life; and see *Intellect: Mind Over Matter* (1990), Part IV, on intellectual virtue: the use, misuse, and nonuse of the intellect.

mum bonum. Leisuring is learning in all the ways that human beings can learn and perfect themselves intellectually; and since human beings are by nature learning animals that have intellects as their highest power, it follows that the perfection of the intellect through all forms of learning is the *summum bonum* that all human beings should desire.

The life of chattel slaves, peasants or serfs in an agricultural economy, factory workers on a subsistence wage working ten to twelve hours a day, seven days a week, was a poor life indeed. It was a life consumed by barely compensated toil, relieved by sleep and little playful recreation. Yet it was the life of millions of human beings in the most advanced countries of the world in the years before the end of the nineteenth century. This is the lowest grade of human life, hardly human at all.

Better, but still far from being a humanly good life, is the life now of those who spend most of their days in working for a good living, productively occupied only with economic goods, ameliorated somewhat by indulgence in recreational play and amusements. The *summum bonum* is not attained by those who are motivated mainly by wealth and pleasure. Though they have plenty of free time not consumed by work and sleep, they kill that surplus time by all the forms of recreation and play that are miscalled "leisure activities" and that have nothing at all to do with genuine leisuring. This is a higher grade of human life, but still not good enough.

The good life, enriched by the *summum bonum* among all the other real goods that constitute the *totum bonum*, is one that involves a decent economic livelihood, the pleasures of play, freedom and political liberty, and the joys of friendship; in addition, it is one that is greatly enriched by spending the greater part of one's free time in the pursuits of leisure, all of which contribute to the growth of the mind and to the attainment of intellectual excellence. This is the highest grade of human life.

These leisure pursuits may be as lowly as gardening, cooking, or cabinetmaking (all of which require skill or art) or as elevated as scientific research, musical composition, or philosophical thought. Relative to the varying degrees of intellectual potential in different individuals, the pursuits of leisure for each individual should take the form of the greatest intellectual accomplishment of which that individual is capable.

Substituting the second and third of these three grades of life for what, in Aristotle's terms, were the political and the philosophical life, the main points in Book X, Chapters 7 and 8, of the *Nicomachean Ethics* are thus preserved by being thus restated in democratic terms.

In the next century, it is to be hoped that democracy and socialism together will reign triumphant in all the technologically advanced countries of the world.[9] The external conditions requisite for leading good human lives of the highest grade will then be available to all. But these ideal conditions will be well used only by those whose conduct is motivated by right desires.

9. For the grounds of this hope, see my book *Haves Without Have-Nots: Essays for the 21st Century on Democracy and Socialism* (1991).

CHAPTER 5

FUNDAMENTAL ERRORS IN MORAL PHILOSOPHY

1

IN WRITING THIS BOOK, I have found it difficult not to anticipate what I would like to set forth systematically and explicitly in this chapter. In the Prologue and in the preceding chapters I have here and there made brief mention of errors in moral philosophy made in modern times by David Hume, Immanuel Kant, John Stuart Mill, and John Dewey. To the mistakes by modern thinkers must be added a mistake made in antiquity by Plato and by the Stoic philosopher Epictetus.

Acquaintance with errors and the correction of them is indispensable to a full understanding of the truth. Accepting and espousing the truth to be found in Aristotle's *Ethics* without being cognizant of the views that are contrary to it and without being able to refute them represents a slender and insufficient grasp of Aristotle's thought. That understanding needs enlargement and enrichment by dealing dialectically with the philosophers whose thinking led them to contrary conclusions.

The error made by David Hume, I have adverted to. His account of what has come to be called the "naturalistic fallacy" can be summarized in two sentences. (1) Our descriptive knowledge of matters of fact, even if it were complete, gives us no basis for affirming the truth of prescriptive imperatives—statements of what ought or ought not to be desired and done. (2) That being the case, an ethics that is deontological rather than teleological, i.e., an ethics of moral obligation rather than one of expediency, is impossible.[1]

The first proposition is true, but the second does not follow from the first. It is a non sequitur. There need be only one self-evident, categorical imperative which combined with true statements of fact validates true prescriptive conclusions. "You ought to desire everything that is really good for you, and nothing else ought to be desired" is the required self-evident, categorical imperative. It is derived from Aristotle's conception of right desire and from his distinction between real and apparent goods.[2]

With the "naturalistic fallacy" disposed of, we turn now to the idealist error first made by Plato and shared later by the Roman Stoics, Immanuel Kant, and other modern philosophers; the rationalist error that is peculiar to Kant, and the Kantians; the utilitarian error made by John Stuart Mill under the influence of Jeremy Bentham; and the realist error made by John Dewey.

----- 2 -----

That having moral virtue is an ideal to be aimed at cannot be called a mistake on Plato's part. But to assert that moral

---

1. See Appendix I, Note 7 for Hume's statement on this point.
2. See *Ten Philosophical Mistakes* (1985), pp. 117–121. Hume's error with regard to the "naturalistic fallacy" leads, in the twentieth century, to the false view that ethics is noncognitive, not a body of valid, objective knowledge of values and obligations.

virtue by itself is sufficient—the only good to be sought—
is the serious mistake that I have called the idealist error.

Plato appears to make that mistake in a single sentence
in the closing words of his *Apology*, his account of the trial
of Socrates. There Socrates, having been condemned to
death by a jury of his fellow citizens in Athens, says to them,
"Know ye that no harm can come to a good man in this
life or the next."

Here is my understanding of that statement. A good man
is a man of good moral character, one who has moral virtue.
He cannot be harmed because there are no other goods of
which he can be deprived. His being allowed to live is not
a good, nor is his being put to death, justly or unjustly, the
deprivation of a good. There may be other interpretations
of the statement I have quoted from Socrates' peroration,
but I am here only contending that, if my interpretation is
correct, Socrates made a mistake.

It is very much to the point that, earlier in Plato's *Apology*,
Socrates made a statement that directly contradicts his closing statement, as I have interpreted it. There he says that
"virtue does not come from wealth, but from virtue comes
wealth and all the other goods." The virtue he is talking
about is moral virtue, and so the statement must be interpreted as asserting that moral virtue is not the only good,
but that there are many other goods, such as wealth and
wisdom, of which a man can be deprived and, being deprived
of them, be injured or harmed.

Certainly, in other Platonic dialogues, Plato gives support
to the view that there are goods other than moral virtue. In
the *Philebus*, Socrates argues against the error of those who
claim that pleasure is the only good, by asking whether it
is better to have both pleasure and wisdom than just to have
pleasure alone.

Also in the first book of the *Republic*, Plato begins his exploration of the idea of justice by presenting an initial definition of doing injustice as injuring or harming another person whether that person is or is not a morally virtuous human being. If no harm can come to a morally virtuous person, it follows that he cannot be injured by unjust treatment.

However, Plato was a philosopher who was sensitive to contradictions, Hence it is reasonable to suppose that he did not himself make the idealist error I have attributed to him on the basis of the statement made by Socrates in his peroration at his trial. But that does not change the fact that other philosophers, notably Epictetus and Immanuel Kant, made the error I may have wrongly attributed to Plato.

In his *Enchiridion*, Epictetus repeatedly declares that nothing external to the will of an individual is intrinsically good or evil. With regard to all things external to our will, we are free to evaluate them as either good or evil. At the end of his little treatise, quoting Plato as his authority, Epictetus asserts that a good will—a righteous or morally virtuous will—is the only thing in the world that has intrinsic goodness and is indispensable to a person's happiness.

The contradiction that Epictetus does not seem to notice lies in the fact that he also thinks of a morally virtuous man as one who, out of a righteous will, acts justly toward others. But how can injustice be done to others if they choose to think that assaulting them, deceiving them, even enslaving them, does not harm them because all these impinging externals can have no effect on their inviolate will.[3]

Centuries later, Kant explicitly repeats the Stoic view of intrinsic good and evil. He declares that the only intrinsic

3. See Appendix I, Note 8.

good is a good or righteous will, one that discharges its moral obligations and leads a man to do his duty. This by itself suffices for a man to lead a morally good life and, thereby, to deserve happiness.

—— 3 ——

The mistake peculiar to Kant is what I have called the rationalist error. It consists in thinking that, without regard to the facts of human nature and without any consideration of the circumstances affecting one's choices or actions, reason and reason alone provides the foundations of moral philosophy.

Reason does so by formulating a categorical imperative that should govern all our conduct: *So act that the maxim of your conduct can become a universal law or rule.* Later philosophers have called this the "generalization principle" or the "universalability thesis." It means simply that you act rightly if the rule that governs your action is also a rule that should govern the action of everyone else. Even more simply stated, that is the Golden Rule: *Do unto others what you would have them do unto you.*

On the face of it, that would appear to be a reasonable prescription. But upon closer examination, it turns out to be an empty one. In the first place, it says nothing at all about what you ought to do for your own sake; and, above all, for your own ultimate good, which is happiness, not conceived psychologically as Kant conceived it, but ethically as Aristotle did. The Golden Rule is concerned only with your actions as affecting others, not with your desires as affecting yourself.

In the second place, how could you do unto others what you would have them do unto you, unless you knew what was really good for you and, being really good, was also really good for every other human being by reason of being an object of natural human desire?

Without reference to the desires that are inherent in human nature, the Golden Rule is devoid of ethical content. It is erroneously concerned with what is right in regard to others without any concern with what is good for everyone. We should be primarily but not exclusively concerned with what is good for everyone; and only secondarily and derivatively with how this knowledge directs us in acting rightly toward others.

Not only is Kant's rationally formulated categorical imperative, like the Golden Rule, devoid of ethical content, but any attempt to give it ethical content must surreptitiously introduce notions about what is really good. In other words, the purity of its rationalism must be polluted by considering the facts of human nature and natural desires.

In addition, the purity of Kant's rationalism does not allow for any casuistry that justifies exceptions to rules by an empirical consideration of the circumstances in a particular case.

This makes Kant's moral philosophy thoroughly dogmatic. The specific rules of conduct he derives from his categorical imperative are rules without any justifiable exceptions, instead of being, as they should be, merely general rules that have justifiable exceptions. To think about moral problems in this way is sheer dogmatism.

One example of such dogmatism will suffice. Kant asserts that the maxim of conduct that forbids us to tell lies follows from his categorical imperative. It is an absolutely universal

rule and allows for no exceptions arising from the circumstances of particular cases. It applies, he tells us, to the
individual who, standing at his fence, sees a man running
desperately from pursuers. The fugitive comes to a fork in
the road and takes the path to the right. Shortly thereafter,
the thugs pursuing him, brandishing clubs and knives with
murderous intent, ask the farmer at the fence which fork in
the road the man running away took.

According to Kantian ethics, the farmer at the fence has
no alternative but to tell the thugs the truth. There is no
justification for his telling them a lie, not even if he knows
or thinks, without a doubt, that the pursuers are murderous
thugs and the fugitive is innocent of any crime. For Kant
there are no white lies. No intentional deception of another
is ever justifiable.[4]

---- **4** ----

It is not the confused and erroneous hedonism of John Stuart
Mill's *Utilitarianism* with which I am here concerned. That
was criticized in Chapter 3, in which we encountered the
wrong desire for pleasure as the only good and clarified the
ambiguity of the word "please" as used by Mill in Chapters
2 and 3 of his book. Here the errors to which I wish to call
attention are in his fourth chapter entitled "Of What Sort
of Proof the Principle of Utility Is Susceptible.[5]

4. See Appendix I, Note 9.
5. Mill calls himself an Epicurean with regard to pleasure. This may be true
of Bentham, whose felicific calculus is clearly hedonistic. But Mill treats pleasure more frequently as the satisfaction of desire rather than as an object of
desire. This treatment of pleasure is more Aristotelian than Epicurean. However, for Mill, all desires are wants, with no distinction between wants and needs.

Before I do so, it should be noted that in Chapter 4, Mill adopts what appears to be the Aristotelian view of happiness as the final and ultimate end that all men desire. "Human nature," Mill writes, "is so constituted as to desire nothing which is not either a part of happiness or a means of happiness. We can have no other proof, and we require no other that these are the only thing desirable."

Apart from the fact that Mill thinks of happiness as the maximization of pleasures enjoyed, the agreement with Aristotle about happiness as the *totum bonum* and ultimate end is superficial. It is little more than an agreement about how the word "happiness" is used by everyone to signify that which is desired for its own sake, not as a means toward anything beyond itself. It signifies that which leaves nothing more to be desired.

That is as far as Mill's agreement with Aristotle goes. Unlike Aristotle, he does not define happiness as activity in accordance with virtue in a complete life, accompanied by wealth and other external goods that are partly the goods of fortune. Nor does he recognize that human beings have a moral obligation to seek their happiness, properly conceived as a morally good life, a life well lived and enriched by the possession of all the real goods that are objects of right desire.

Aristotle as well as Kant would reject Mill's moral philosophy on the grounds that it is purely teleological and pragmatic—an ethics of means and ends which, like Jeremy Bentham's felicific calculus, contains no moral prescriptions using the words "ought" and "ought not." We are not under the obligation to pursue that which is rightly desired; we are left to calculate what means to employ in order to achieve the end that pleases us most. Its principles are principles of expediency and of results, not of right desire and of obligations to be fulfilled.[6]

Passing over all of Mill's mistakes about pleasure and happiness and his recourse to subjective feelings as the ultimate source of discrimination between what is more or less desirable, the central error in *Utilitarianism* is its proposal of two final ends that can come into conflict. One is the individual's own happiness. The other is what Mill calls "the general happiness"—the happiness of all other human beings who are one's fellows in a given society, usually miscalled "the greatest good of the greatest number."

On the one hand, Mill proposes as a self-evident truth that the individual's own happiness is the ultimate end at which the inborn tendencies of human nature do, in fact, aim. On the other hand, he proposes what he calls "the general happiness" (i.e., the happiness of others) as the ultimate goal.

Two ultimate goals, two final ends, on the face of it, are impossible. Recognizing the possibility of conflict between two such goals, Mill subordinates the individual's own happiness to the general happiness and allows himself to slip into a prescriptive judgment that we *should* aim at the general happiness even if that does not also serve the purpose of procuring for ourselves our own individual happiness.

The problem he has created for himself, Mill fails to solve. The only final end and ultimate goal that the individual should seek is that individual's own happiness. But when happiness is properly defined as the ultimate good that befits our common nature it is obviously a common good, the same for all members of the human species.

6. See Appendix I, Note 10.

As I pointed out in Chapter 4, the phrase "common good" has another meaning: the good of the organized community in which the individual lives. The happiness that is *common* to all human individuals is the *bonum commune hominis*. The general, social welfare, the public good, the good of the community (*bonum commune communitatis*) is also a common good, but *common* in a different sense— not common because it is the same for all individuals, but common because all members of the community can participate in it.

The problem Mill failed to solve can be solved only by making all these distinctions. The happiness of others depends upon the good of the community in which they live. Their participation in that common good enables them to obtain real goods that are parts of or means to their own individual happiness.

For each individual, the good of the community in which he lives is a means to his or her own happiness. Conversely, each individual in acting for his or her own individual happiness cannot help but work for the public common good that serves the happiness of others as well as his or her own individual happiness, since that happiness is common to or the same in all.

Thus, there are not two ultimate goals, but only one. The general happiness, the happiness of others, is not an ultimate goal for the individual. He acts for it indirectly when, in acting for his own individual happiness, he also acts for the public common good (that is not only a means to his own happiness, but also a means to the happiness of all others who participate in it.[7]

7. See Appendix I, Note 11.

—— 5 ——

Like Mill's *Utilitarianism,* John Dewey's *Human Nature and Conduct* is thoroughly pragmatic—a teleological ethics of means and ends, devoid of any prescriptive judgments about what human beings ought to desire and do.

As for Mill, so for Dewey, facts about human nature provide a basis for his ethics. To that extent, it has an Aristotelian cast. In Dewey's case, not only does human nature play a central role, but he also gives the notion of habit a crucial position in his moral philosophy.

Thus, in its teleological aspect, in its reliance on an understanding of human nature, and in its giving prime importance to the habitual dispositions of human beings, not to their singular actions, Dewey's moral philosophy is Aristotelian in tenor.

What, then, is its chief defect—the realist error that makes Dewey's moral philosophy a purely descriptive ethics, devoid of prescriptions? It consists in Dewey's denial of any goal in human life that is a final and ultimate end that all human beings ought to seek, as well as all the means they ought to seek in order to attain it in a complete life.[8]

For Dewey, while individuals are still alive, every end they in fact do seek is always a means to some further end. Nothing is ever sought except as a means to some further end that, in turn, is a means to some further end, and so on, until death is the end that terminates all further seeking.

Dewey's error lies in his failure to distinguish between terminal and normative ends. Death is a terminal end, not a normative end. It is a terminal end that few individuals

8. See Appendix I, Note 12.

do, in fact, seek. Dewey is correct in thinking that, in this life, death is the only terminal end. But there are goals that momentarily serve as terminal ends; for example, when we travel and set a city as our destination, that city is for the time being a terminal end. When we reach it, the desire that motivated our travel is quieted. But we may then wish to travel further and set another city as our destination, using where we are as a means to getting there.

All terminal ends or goals must be attained before they are used as means to further ends or goals. In both respects, a normative goal differs from a terminal goal. An ultimate end that is normative rather than terminal is a goal that is never momentarily attained and later used as a means. Happiness, psychologically conceived as the state of contentment at any moment when one gets everything one wants, is a terminal goal. Happiness, ethically conceived as a whole life well lived and as the ultimate good that all human beings ought to desire, is the final end that is a normative goal.

We can understand the difference between terminal and normative goals by considering the difference between the performing arts and the arts that produce things that have enduring existence, such as the shoe the cobbler makes, the house the architect builds, or the ship the shipwright constructs.

A symphony performed by an orchestra may take an hour to play. From start to finish, it is continually coming into being and passing away. The whole of it does not exist at any moment in the course of its being played.

The conductor who aims to play the symphony as well as possible is, therefore, aiming at a goal that is normative, not terminal. It is a goal that controls and governs how the symphony should be conducted in every phase of its development. Only when the playing of the symphony has been completed, can anyone judge that it has been well played and that the conductor has succeeded in discharging his obligation to play it well.

Banal as the comparison may appear to be, achieving a well-lived life—achieving happiness as ethically conceived—is like playing a symphony well. It is a normative, not a terminal, goal. It is the goal of right desire for which all the means should be rightly chosen.

I have drawn on the main distinctions, principles, and conclusions in Aristotle's *Ethics* in order to point out these four fundamental errors in moral philosophy. But in doing so I have not given readers a documented exposition of Aristotle's *Ethics*, so that they can become cognizant of how that book presents the truths I have borrowed from it, sometimes reformulating them in slightly different terms, sometimes embellishing them, and sometimes adding a point or a distinction that may be helpful to contemporary readers.[9]

---

9. See Appendix II for an annotated commentary on Aristotle's *Ethics*. This is the Postscript to *The Time of Our Lives* (1970), now out of print.

CHAPTER 6

NECESSARY BUT NOT SUFFICIENT

1

Right thinking is less than enough for habitual right desire. It may be necessary for the acknowledgment of moral problems, and even for some understanding of how they can be solved; but it is insufficient for their solution. It does not produce moral virtue, or the habit of right desire, which is an indispensable means to living well.

In turn, moral virtue is necessary, but it is also by itself insufficient for the successful pursuit of happiness, ethically conceived. Having the habit of right desire, which is moral virtue, must be present as a necessary condition for human beings to act righteously for the most part, but it is insufficient to guarantee that result.

Why are all these things true? As to the first, because a person can know and understand the truths of moral philosophy without possessing the habit of right desire that constitutes a virtuous character. That reason, by the way, is the reason why Aristotle said it was futile to give lectures on ethics to the young, the immature.

The reason why persons of good moral character may infrequently commit wrong acts is that we have two kinds of desire—sensitive or sensual desires, and rational desires that are acts of the intellectual appetite, which is the will. These two kinds of desire often operate simultaneously in particular cases, but they seldom act cooperatively, but rather in conflict.[1]

When this occurs and virtuous individuals succumb to the sensual desires, which motivate them to act contrary to their rational desires, Aristotle calls the wrong actions that then result acts of incontinence. Incontinence is the reason why having a habit of right desire does not guarantee that persons of good character always act as they should. Moral virtue is necessary but insufficient.

A more important reason why moral virtue is necessary but insufficient is that it is not the only factor required for the pursuit of happiness as the ultimate goal of right desire. The other factor required is good luck, or what Aristotle calls "the blessings of good fortune." Like moral virtue it is necessary, but also insufficient.

Let us now examine these three factors, which are insufficient or less than enough that is needed for solving moral problems and leading a good life.

----- 2 -----

We are indebted to Plato for the insight that moral virtue is not teachable. His dialogue the *Meno* opens with the

1. For the psychological account of these two kinds of desire and of the conflict between them in particular acts of choice, see my discussion of willing and choosing in Chapter 14 of *Intellect: Mind Over Matter* (1990), especially pp. 164–169.

question "whether [moral] virtue is acquired by teaching or by practice; or if neither by teaching nor practice, then whether it comes to man by nature, or in what other way."

The dialogue contains a good example of teaching, in which Socrates teaches a slave boy how to learn the solution of a problem in geometry. Clearly, moral virtue cannot be acquired in the way in which such knowledge is learned, certainly not by the asking and answering of questions, nor by lecturing.

The full reason why this is so does not become clear in Plato's dialogue. It is Aristotle's definition of moral virtue as a habit of choice that helps us to understand why it is not acquired by teaching. The fact that moral virtue is a habit eliminates one of the alternatives mentioned by Plato. Habits are acquired; therefore, moral virtue is not by nature. We are not born virtuous.

The other alternative mentioned by Plato—by practice—comes nearer to the answer. We all know that habits are formed by the repetition of the same action time and time again. Anyone who has practiced playing the piano or another musical instrument is kept at it by the maxim "Practice makes perfect." A well-executed performance results from the habit formed by conscientious and diligent practice.

But are there not music teachers who teach students how to play instruments well? The kind of teaching they do is usually called coaching. They supervise the practice by telling the student, step by step, what to do and what not to do, and as the practicing proceeds, they stop it every time the learner makes a mistake and they require him to do it correctly, over and over again, until the student does it in a satisfactory manner.

On the assumption that the person who is the student wishes to learn, the individual willingly complies with such instruction. At no point does he consider whether he should or should not do what the coach prescribes. He does not exercise any choice about whether he will or will not submit to the advice of the coach and follow the rules laid down.

In that word "choice" lies the answer, especially if the choice is understood to be free choice. Moral virtues are habits of choice, said Aristotle. Habits of choice can be formed only by acts of choice. Those acts of choice are made by individuals when they are confronted with alternatives that solicit their response: this versus that apparent good, this apparent good versus this real good; this versus that real good here and now.

They are motivated to respond by conflicting desires that push or pull them in one direction or another. To act, they must choose in which direction to go. Time and time again, they are confronted with alternatives of the same kind; and by the repeated choices they make, one or another habit is formed. If the habit formed is a habit of right desire, they have acquired moral virtue.

Cannot a coach teach moral virtue in the way that a music teacher coaches playing an instrument? Do not parents or other elders do something like coaching when they tell their young charges which choice to make with respect to moral alternatives confronting them? Do they not try to use the carrot and the stick—rewards and punishments—to reinforce their advice and to win compliance? Do they not sometimes resort to models of right choice with the hope that the attractiveness of the example will solicit imitations of it? Do they not also tell stories of their own misbehavior and point out the regrettable consequences to which it led, concluding with the admonition "Don't do what I did and you'll be making the right choice"?

Yes, parents and other tutors of the young in moral matters do all these things in their effort to form habits of right choice in the young and thereby good character. Why, then, do they not succeed in teaching moral virtue to the same degree that teachers of geometry can succeed with students able and willing to learn geometry?

We all know that they do not succeed with the same degree of regularity. Parents with a number of children, trying to form their characters in approximately the same way, succeed with some of them and fail with some of them. They do not have the same assurance that the teacher of geometry has that they should be able to succeed with all.

The answer lies in the freedom of choice that the young exercise when they are subject to coaching in moral matters. Free choice consists in always being able to choose otherwise, no matter how one chooses. If the choices that the individual makes in the process of habit formation were not free choices, the habit formed would not be a habit of virtue or vice.[2]

Herein lies the difference between moral virtue and vice and the intellectual virtues, such as knowledge (e.g., knowledge of geometry). In the one case, the habit is formed by repeated free choices, either right or wrong. In the other case, given the initial willingness of the student to learn geometry, further compliance with the teacher's instruction ceases to be a matter of free choice.

Presented with true and false alternatives, the student's intellect is necessitated to affirm what is true and reject what is false. Not so in the case of moral matters: the will is not

---

2. If virtue and vice were not freely formed habits of choice, they would not be meritorious and reprehensible. Praise and blame should not be given for human traits that are either natural endowments or formed by the compulsion or necessitation of circumstances. The traits may be admirable or not, but they are not praiseworthy or blameworthy if they could not have been otherwise.

necessitated by either of the alternatives presented. That is just another way of saying that it has freedom of choice.

Little more need be said about why moral virtue cannot be taught in the same way that geometry is taught or in the same way that musical performance is coached. This does not preclude the usefulness of giving the young counsel and advice, the guidance of models and examples, the persuasion of rewards and punishments. It merely points out why all these devices have no assurance of success.

What about the teaching of moral philosophy or ethics as a prescriptive science? If ethics is, as I affirm it to be, a body of validly objective knowledge, it certainly can be taught in the same way that other sciences are taught. Should it be taught for the purpose of producing persons of good moral character? Here the full answer is neither certain nor clear.

Returning to the point that initiated this discussion, one part of the answer is now clear. A person who has learned the truths of moral philosophy has acquired knowledge that by itself is insufficient for that individual's acquirement of a good moral character. Knowing the truths of moral philosophy, a person may still turn out to be a knave or a villain.

Knowledge and understanding are intellectual virtues. No one disputes the fact that a person can have intellectual virtues to a high degree without being a person of admirable moral character. A college student of philosophy can pass a course in ethics with a high grade and at the same time exhibit disgraceful habits of desire and action.

Learning the truths of moral philosophy may be insufficient for the acquirement of moral virtue, but is it necessary even though insufficient? The fact that persons entirely innocent of moral philosophy are often persons of good moral character shows that it cannot be necessary. While not necessary, it may be still be recommended not merely because the pursuit of truth is always commendable, but also because understanding the truths of moral philosophy reinforces right desire when it is challenged by the temptations of seductive apparent goods that should be shunned.

———— 3 ————

Is there anyone who has not experienced remorse for having made a wrong choice or committed a wrong deed? How is it that we can know what is right and not choose it, or know what is wrong and still do it?

The words used in the confession of sins are clear on this point. "We have done the things we ought not to have done, and we have failed to do what we ought to have done." When Socrates said that knowledge is virtue, he asserted the opposite. Our knowing what is right necessitates our doing what is right. Therein lies the error made by Socrates.

As I intimated earlier, Aristotle's analysis of incontinence in Book VII of his *Ethics* supplies us with the answer. We have two kinds of desire, not one: sensual desires and rational desires, desires of the intellectual appetite or will. They frequently come into conflict with one another, as most of us know from personal experience or from the vicarious experience of reading novels or seeing dramas in which the conflict between reason and the passions is central to the narrative or action.

We make important choices many times in the course of our lives. They are always made at a particular time and place and under particular circumstances. The alternatives with which we are confronted simultaneously may be objects of sensual desire, on the one hand, and objects of rational desire, on the other hand.

Intellectually knowing what is really good for us to choose, our intellectual appetite or will tends toward the objects of rational desire. Attributing apparent goodness to sensually attractive objects, our sensitive desires tend toward those objects.

When the objects of rational desire are remote real goods—goods that cannot be obtained at the moment of choice—and the objects of sensitive desire are sensually present apparent goods, obtainable here and now, it is easy to give in to the temptations of immediately obtainable goods and hard to postpone the gratification of desire by choosing goods that are obtainable only in the long run.

When persons make choices they later regret, or suffer remorse for choices they failed to make, what Aristotle called their incontinence consists in their refusal to defer gratification. He also tells us that the urge toward immediate gratification of desire is a typically childish indulgence in pleasures, meaning thereby not only the pleasures of the flesh, but also the pleasures that consist in being pleased when we get the things we want at the moment we want them.

Acquiring moral virtue, forming the habit of right desire, is thus seen to be a process of conquering one's childish tendencies toward indulgence in immediate gratifications.

This is not a complete account of all conflicts between reason and the passions. Objects of desire are not always pleasures of the flesh, or even objects that are immediately obtainable and pleasing in the sense that they satisfy our desires. Money, fame, and power are not objects of this sort. Nevertheless, they arouse passions which drive us to make wrong choices.

The fourth book of Spinoza's *Ethics* is entitled "Of the passions or of human bondage." The freedom we have lost when we are in bondage to the passions is the freedom of being able to will as we ought. That freedom is enjoyed only by persons of moral virtue. They have acquired that freedom by acquiring the habit of right choice, the habit of willing as one ought.

4

In a treatise on happiness or the good life, Augustine declared that happy is the person who, in the course of a complete life, has satisfied all desires, *provided that the individual desired nothing amiss*. If desiring nothing amiss is having the habit of right desire, then Augustine's declaration is another statement of a mistake we have already discussed—the error of thinking that moral virtue is not only necessary but also sufficient for happiness or leading a good life.

Aristotle would correct Augustine's error by adding another proviso. He would say that happiness consists in a complete life in which all one's desires are satisfied provided (a) the individual desires nothing amiss and also provided (b) that goods which are not wholly within the power of individuals to obtain for themselves are obtained partly as the result of good luck or the blessings of good fortune.

The second proviso is expressed in the definition of happiness that Aristotle formulates in Chapter 10 of Book I of his *Ethics*. There he says that happiness is attained only in a complete life; that it involves activity in accordance with moral virtue; and that it also must be accompanied by a moderate possession of wealth. Since wealth is an external good, a possession rather than a personal perfection, such as the virtues, moral and intellectual, we can correctly expand the mention of wealth to include other external goods.

External goods are goods that are never wholly within our power to obtain for ourselves. Good luck or the blessings of good fortune may bestow them upon us or help us to obtain them. The benefactions of just government secure for us or help us to obtain the real goods to which we have a natural and unalienable human right.

Being the citizen of a society the government of which is distributively just is certainly a blessing of good fortune. It is a blessing that does not befall a large part of the human race.

It is not only external goods, such as wealth, that are not wholly within the power of individuals to obtain for themselves, and so depend for their attainment either upon good luck or upon the benefactions of a just government. What is true of wealth is also true of health, of liberty, of knowledge, even of friendships; in fact, of all real goods except moral virtue, and of many innocuous apparent goods as well. Except for moral virtue, which is wholly within our power to acquire by free choice, all other goods partly depend on external circumstances—on the condition of the physical environment in which one happens to live and on the institutions and enactments of the government under which one happens to live.

The truth we have just considered can be briefly summarized by saying that there are two indispensable conditions requisite for happiness, ethically conceived. One is moral virtue. The other is good luck, or the blessings of good fortune. Both are necessary conditions, but neither by itself is a sufficient condition.

The lives of persons having moral virtue can be blemished and, even in extreme cases, ruined by the adversities of outrageous fortune. Persons having all the blessings of good fortune can ruin their own lives or seriously blemish them by the vices to which they are addicted.

Aristotle is the only moral philosopher in the Western tradition who makes good luck as well as moral virtue a necessary condition of a life that is morally good as well as one that is enriched by the attainment of all real goods and many apparent goods that are innocuous. That is why I think his *Ethics* is the only sound and pragmatic moral philosophy that has made its appearance in the last twenty-five centuries.

If this unique feature of Aristotle's *Ethics* were not true, all the social, political, and economic reforms that have occurred in the last twenty-five centuries would be shorn of meaning and purpose. They were all instituted and enacted in order to bestow upon human beings the external conditions they need for a good human life. If moral virtue were sufficient for the successful pursuit of happiness, human beings could lead good human lives under the deprivations imposed upon them by the deplorable conditions under which a great many still live.

The goal at which a just government should aim would not be the happiness of all its citizens. That would be entirely within their own power to pursue by acquiring moral virtue.

Morally virtuous chattel slaves and morally virtuous disfranchised females could lead good human lives; so, too, could those living in dire poverty or suffering from serious illness without adequate medical care.

In the lives of most of us, there is an imperfection that only the most fortunate completely escape. Most of us suffer personal tragedies in which we are confronted with having to choose between alternatives, neither or which is desirable or good. We are thus compelled to take unto ourselves, by free choice, an evil that we would otherwise strive to avoid.

EPILOGUE
Transcultural Ethics

1

IN A BOOK ENTITLED *Truth in Religion: The Plurality of Religions and the Unity of Truth* (1990), I addressed myself to the problem of transculturality. The first chapter, on "The Restriction of Pluralism," distinguished between matters of truth and matters of taste, then argued that pluralism was necessary and right in all matters of taste, but not at all in any matter concerned with factual and logical truth. In all such matters, whatever objective truth can be attained should also be universal. If so, it is transcultural.

At this juncture in history, mathematics, the exact natural sciences (physics, cosmology, chemistry), and their dependent technologies have become transcultural. Not so the social sciences, history, and philosophy.

We are here concerned only with the question about whether philosophy is in the realm of truth or in the realm of taste, along with all other matters of opinion and personal predilection. Ethics is a branch of philosophy. To ask whether ethics should become transcultural is to ask whether the judgments made in ethics about what is really good for human beings and about the ultimate goal they should seek and the means they should choose to attain it have objective and universal truth.

The central theses of this book call for an affirmative answer. I have shown how prescriptive judgments have truth, a different kind of truth than that of the descriptive judgments made in the natural sciences. I have shown that all desires for the goods our human natures need are right desires. I have shown that, among the merely apparent goods, which are the objects of our acquired desires, some are innocuous and some noxious, and that it is permissible to desire the innocuous apparent good and add them to the real goods we need in our pursuit of happiness.

I have explained that when we cease to use the word "happiness" for a psychological state of contentment and use it, in its ethical sense, for a whole life, lived in accordance with moral virtue and enriched by the cumulative possession of all real goods, happiness or the good life is the same ultimate goal to be sought by all human beings, differing from individual to individual only with respect to the innocuous apparent goods that enter into it.

If these prescriptive propositions are objectively true, they are also universally true. If they are universally true, then the moral philosophy that contains these prescriptive judgments is transcultural. The only descriptive propositions that are presupposed by this reasoning and underlie its validity are the propositions that mankind is defined by having a specific human nature; and that all members of the human species have exactly the same nature, differing superficially in the habits that have been formed by the different cultures in which they have lived, and the different environmental circumstances that have had impact on their development.

These presupposed propositions run contrary to the denial of a specific human nature by twentieth-century existentialists and by the cultural anthropologists of our time. In their view, a transcultural ethics is impossible. All moral judgments are ethnocentric.

Hence to support the validity of the opposite claim it is necessary to expose the serious error they have made in failing to distinguish the innate endowments common to all human beings from their acquired nurtural and cultural modifications. They have mistakenly supposed that these nurtural and cultural modifications, differing from one ethnic subgroup of the human species to another, are, in effect, their differing natures.

Accordingly, what befits the traits of one ethnic subgroup does not befit the traits of another. What one ethnic subgroup needs or wants in the way of goods, or how it thinks about what is right and wrong, provides them with no basis for adversely judging the needs and wants or the value judgments that are ethnocentric. They do not and cannot have objective and universal truth.

I have, in recent books, tried to explain and refute the mistake made by the existentialists and the cultural anthropologists, never made before the twentieth century.[1] Since the crucial premise in reasoning that reaches an affirmative conclusion concerning transcultural ethics is the proposition that the specific nature of all human beings is the same, that their natural needs are all the same, and that their minds are essentially alike, I recommend that readers acquaint

1. See *Ten Philosophical Mistakes* (1985), Chapter 8; and *Intellect: Mind Over Matter* (1990), Chapters 10 and 11.

themselves with the arguments pro and con before they themselves decide whether ethics should or should not be transcultural.

2

In a much earlier book, *The Time of Our Lives* (1970), which is now out of print, I discussed, in Chapter 12, individual and cultural differences with respect to the pursuit of happiness in its ethical sense—in what respects it is the same for all human beings and in what respects if differs from one individual to another and from one culture to another. I think it may be helpful to readers of the present book if I add here an abbreviated excerpt from that chapter:

> It may be useful to reiterate three points that have been made about a whole life that is really good, or about happiness when that is identical in meaning with a really good life. The first is that, being the *totum bonum*, it omits nothing that is really good and so leaves no need unfulfilled, no natural desire unsatisfied.[2]
>
> The second is that happiness or a whole good life can never be experienced at any moment or period during the course of living, though the exercise of memory and imagination does enable us to consider our life as a whole. We can never say, during a man's life, that he is happy, any more

2. To say that a life made good by the possession of all real goods leaves no natural desire unsatisfied does not imply the complete or perfect satisfaction of all natural desires. For example, it is unlikely that man's natural desire for knowledge can ever be fully satisfied in the course of this earthly life. It follows, therefore, that the achievement of the *totum bonum* is a matter of degree. All the real goods must be present in a good life, but they need not be present to the same degree.

than we can say, before his life is over, that he has succeeded in making a good life for himself, since while he is still alive, his whole life is still in the process of becoming.

In view of this we can say of a man who is succeeding in the task of making a good life for himself only that he is *becoming* happy or, in other words, that he is on his way to doing the job, but he has not yet finished doing it.[3] This is the profound insight that lies concealed in the phrase "pursuit of happiness" and, as we shall see, this also explains why the basic natural right that a just society or government should try to secure—and aid or abet—for every individual is not, and cannot be, the right to happiness, but it is rather the right to its pursuit.

One way of remembering this point is to remember the qualification that must be added to the famous definition of happiness given by Boethius. He said: Happiness consists in the possession in aggregate of all good things—all the things that are really good for a man.[4]

The qualification that must be added is that life being a temporal whole, and a good life something that can be made only in the course of using up the time of our lives, the possession of all good things can be achieved only successively and cumulatively—from day to day, and from

3. In the context of his statement that a man achieves happiness through gaining all the things he desires, *provided that he desire nothing amiss*, Augustine adds a further observation relevant to the point that a man cannot be called happy in the course of his life, since happiness is the quality of a whole life that is good. A man, Augustine writes, can be called "almost happy who desires well, for good things make a man happy, and such a man already possesses some good—namely, a good will" (*On the Trinity*, Book XIII, Chapter 6). I would say that the man who has a virtuous or good will, one that is habitually disposed "to desire nothing amiss," possesses the principal operative or functional means for becoming happy. I would not say that he is "almost happy," but rather that he is on the road toward making a good life for himself. His possession of a virtuous will increases the probability that he will succeed in his efforts, but it does not ensure his success, for other factors beyond his control may impede or defeat his pursuit of happiness.
4. See *The Consolation of Philosophy*, Book III, Chapter 2.

year to year; it cannot be achieved in this life by the simultaneous presence of all good things at a single moment in time.

The third point is that a good life can include apparent goods of all sorts—things that men want even if they have no natural need for them and even if they cannot be rationally justified as necessary for achieving a good life. But this is true only with the stringent qualification or restriction that the apparent goods a man goes after, or the way he goes after them to satisfy his wants, do not in any way conflict with his getting all the real goods he needs, or with getting them to the fullest extent to which they are really good for him.

In other words, the moral obligation to make a really good life for oneself does not preclude satisfying one's wants and seeking things that are apparent but not real goods, but only if they are *innocuous—only if* the pursuit of them *does not interfere* with the pursuit of happiness.

The foregoing clarifications and developments of the commonsense view cannot help but elicit from psychologists, sociologists, and cultural anthropologists an objection that was not mentioned earlier when I enumerated the various criticisms that philosophers would level against it. The objection is to the proposition that the *totum bonum*—happiness or a really good life—is the same for all men at all times and all places, and under all circumstances; in consequence of which, all men are under the same moral obligation when it is said that each ought to make a good life for himself.

The empirical psychologist objects to this on the grounds that it ignores the whole range of individual differences in physique, temperament, and talent—intelligence and native endowments or aptitudes. The sociologist or cultural anthropologist objects to this on the similar grounds that it ignores the whole range of societal and cultural differences— differences in all the man-made circumstances that surround an individual life, and perhaps differences in the physical environment as well that often occasion or help to form particular social or cultural institutions.

The reply to both objections is the same. It consists, first, in acknowledging the relevance of all the facts about individual and cultural differences that we either know as a matter of ordinary experience or have learned from investigations conducted by the behavioral scientists. But these are not the only facts to be taken into account.

There is also the preeminent fact that all men belong to the same biological species and, as such, are the same in nature, that is, have the same biological properties, the same basic native capacities—dispositions and needs. When this fact is put together with the facts of individual differences, we see that while the general outlines of a good life are the same for all men because they all have the same specific nature, the details that fill that outline in detail differ from man to man because men all differ individually from one another.

That is one reason why it was said earlier that the plan for making a good life—one that would be a common plan for all men to follow—can only be sketched in its general outlines and cannot be worked out in all its concrete details. The latter can be done only by each individual and only from moment to moment in the course of a whole life.

A few examples may help to make this point clearer. Being the animals they are, all men must devote a portion of their time to the biologically necessary activities we have grouped together under the term *sleep*. But differing from one another in temperament and physique, as well as in external circumstances, they will not all engage in these activities in the *same* way or to the *same* degree.

Similarly, though all men ought to devote as much of their time as possible to *leisure-work*, because they cannot do too much of this for their own good, their individual differences in temperament and talent, as well as in the external circumstances of their lives, will lead them to engage in different types of leisure-work and to engage in them in different ways.

The same holds for *playful activities*, which will differ both in degree and in manner from man to man, because of their individual differences and the differences in the circumstances that affect their lives. And it also holds for *subsistence-work* in the case of those men who, for want of enough wealth or property, are under compulsion to earn a living for themselves.

Hence it is possible to say that happiness or a good life, conceived in its general outlines as the same for all, is attainable by all men, except those who are prevented by abnormal individual disabilities or incapacities or those who are prevented by the extremes of good or bad fortune.

With the exceptions noted, all men have an equal opportunity to attain happiness or to make a good life, but this equality is one of proportionality. Differing individually in their capacities, each can fulfill his capacities to the utmost, and although the degree of happiness attained may not be identical for all, it will be proportionally equal for all who make an equally successful effort.

This does not mean that all men will in fact make the degree of effort they ought to make or that, given differences in circumstances, the same degree of effort will be equally successful. As a result, all men may not achieve happiness or a good life to the fullest degree of which they are individually capable. In addition, quite apart from considerations of degree, the manner in which men engage in the pursuit of happiness will differ from individual to individual.

I said earlier that the same answer applied not only to individual differences, differences in native endowment, but also to societal and cultural differences, all of them environmental and circumstantial. But when we consider differences of the latter sort—the circumstantial differences—one qualification must be added that is not called for in the case of differences in native endowment.

Plato long ago observed that what is honored in a society is cultivated there. It would also seem to be true that what is not honored in a society—or, more emphatically, what is socially or culturally regarded as having little or no worth—cannot be cultivated there.

It may be too much to expect any individual—or any but the rarest exception—to be so extreme a nonconformist that he will earnestly and steadfastly seek for himself things that, while really good for him because he is a man, are not honored by the society in which he lives or, worse, are strongly disapproved of.

The converse of this may also be true; namely, that the individual, conforming to the mores and value system of the society in which he lives, will indulge in activities, or indulge in them to a degree, that lead to results that are not *really* good for him or any other human being, yet are generally *deemed* good by his society or culture.

Consequently, it is highly probable that under certain societal or cultural conditions, it may be extremely difficult, if not impossible, for an individual to satisfy all his natural needs or to attain, to the requisite degree, all the things that are really good for him as a human being.

This being the case, we can judge human societies or

cultures as good and bad, better or worse, in spite of all the injunctions against doing so delivered by the sociologists and cultural anthropologists. The sociologists and cultural anthropologists tell us that we cannot transcend what they call the "ethnocentric predicament" in which we find ourselves. Any judgment we make about a culture other than our own will assume the soundness or validity of the mores and value system of our own society or culture.

This would, of course, be true if *all* value systems were relative and had validity—or acceptance—only for the culture in which they were inherent. However, the value system involved in the scale of real goods that constitute a good human life is relative only to human nature, and not to societies or cultures. As such, it provides a standard that transcends the mores and the diverse value systems that are inherent in diverse cultures. It is a universally applicable standard because it is based on what is universally present in all societies—human beings, the same in their specific nature.[5]

Hence, by applying this standard, it is possible to judge any society or culture as good or bad, better or worse, including our own, and we can do so without falling into the ethnocentric predicament that is the bugaboo of the sociologists and anthropologists.

---

5. If the sociologists and anthropologists were correct about the impossibility of transcending the ethnocentric predicament, not only would they be unable to judge the value systems of other societies and cultures without assuming the validity of their own, they would also be unable objectively to criticize their own society and culture. Yet they are often to be found among the most vocal and extreme critics of the social institutions, the mores, and the value system of their native land. What objective criteria are available to them when they pass moral judgments on things at home which they think that the ethnocentric predicament deprives them of when they refrain from passing similar judgments on things abroad? (See Charles Van Doren, *The Idea of Progress*, especially Chapters 1 and 14.)

A society or culture is good if it does not prevent its members form making a really good life for themselves, and one is better than another if, to a greater degree than that other, it facilitates the pursuit of happiness for all or for more of its members.

A society or culture is bad if it prevents some or all of its members from achieving the *totum bonum* that constitutes a really good human life, and one is worse than another if, to a greater degree than that other, it interferes with the pursuit of happiness for all or for more of its members.

It is by this standard—*there is and can be no other to serve the purpose*—that we must judge the society and culture of the United States in the twentieth century when we come to consider the question whether this is a good time to be alive and whether ours is a good society to be alive in.

---- 3 ----

Do not all human beings rightly desire liberty? Do they not all rightly desire knowledge? Do they not all rightly desire to live in association with other human beings, some of whom they love or regard as friends? Do they not all rightly desire to be treated justly by their associates and by the society in which they live?

Are there any goods that some human beings ought to desire that other human beings ought not to desire? Is there any ultimate goal in human life that some human beings ought to seek that other human beings ought not to seek? Is there any standard of justice that applies to one human society that does not apply to all human societies?

Should not all human beings rightly desire the political

liberty enjoyed by enfranchised citizens in a constitutional democracy? Should not all human beings rightly desire to have a decent livelihood supported by the arrangements under which they live? If so, then the political and economic ideals that are at last being recognized as inseparable ideals to be realized throughout the civilized world are democracy and socialism.[6]

6. See my recent book *Haves Without Have-Nots: Essays for the 21st Century on Democracy and Socialism* (1991).

APPENDIXES

ENDNOTES AND POSTSCRIPT
from *The Time of Our Lives*

(published in 1970 and now out of print)

APPENDIX I

ENDNOTES

Note 1. Pleasure and Procreation as Motives for Sexual Activity

Because sexual morality is a matter of such general interest, it may be useful to say a word more. Let me preface what I am about to say by the observation that in my judgment, as in the judgment of leading liberal Catholic theologians, contraception is not a violation of the natural moral law. The official position of the Vatican rests on the factually false proposition that human sexuality is intended by nature to serve only one end—procreation. If that were so, any form of birth control, whether by mechanical or pharmacological devices or by resorting to the "free period" in the female menstrual cycle, would be against the moral law. But human sexuality serves at least two purposes; one is procreation, the other is the mutual pleasure and even, perhaps, the fulfillment of erotic love on the part of those who are thus united, whether married or not.

The fact that the human female has no estrous cycle like that which governs coupling in most other species of sexual animals, restricting it to the brief period favorable to procreation, is by itself sufficient evidence for the proposition that human sexuality serves other purposes, and this is confirmed by the wide variety of forms human sexuality takes, only some of which are effective for procreation, and none of which can properly be called perverse or unnatural. Those terms would be applicable only if procreation were the sole purpose that human sexual activity was intended by nature to serve.

Aquinas, expressing a view that the Catholic Church still officially adheres to, says that "the emission of the semen ought to be so directed that both the proper generation may ensue and the education of the offspring be secured" or, in other words, copulation should occur only within the bonds of matrimony, so that the possible offspring can be adequately cared for by the family, and it should never occur without the intention of producing offspring.

If this formulation of the moral law with regard to sexual conduct is incorrect, as I have argued that it is, then the correct view of simple fornication is the one that Aquinas states in the following manner: "Given a woman free from a husband, and under no control of father or any other person, if any one approaches her with her consent, he does her no wrong, because she is pleased so to act, and has the disposal of her own person; nor does he do any wrong to another, for she is under no one's control; therefore there appears to be no sin. Nor does it seem to be a sufficient answer to say she wrongs God, for God is not offended by us except by what we do against our own good; but it does not appear that this conduct is against man's good; hence no wrong seems to be done to God thereby. In like manner also it does not appear to be a sufficient answer, that wrong is thereby done one's neighbor, who is scandalized; for sometimes a neighbor is scandalized by what is not a sin" (*Summa Contra Gentiles*, Bk. III, Ch. 122).

The only "sufficient answer" according to Aquinas is the one based on the moral law that sexual congress should be entered into only for the purpose of generating offspring and only under conditions (i.e., matrimony) which provide care for the possible offspring. If we reject this, then, according to Aquinas' own reasoning, there is nothing morally wrong in simple fornication.

Note 2. Temperance in Sexual Behavior

The point made about a habit of lying as bad for the individual leads us to a similar observation about sexual behavior. We have seen that simple fornication is not morally wrong, and also that no sexual acts which yield mutual pleasure to consenting individuals can be condemned as perverse or unnatural. But this must not be interpreted to mean that sexual behavior is subject to no moral restrictions whatsoever. On the contrary, it is subject to the same kind of moral restrictions that are applicable to other forms of playful activity, indulged in for the sake of the pleasure that attends them.

The intemperance that manifests itself in the disposition to prefer the pleasures of the moment to a good life as a whole, or that consists in habitual overindulgence in sensual pleasures, can defeat an individual's pursuit of happiness. While sexual pleasure is a good thing, it is, like many other real goods of that category, a good of which one can want too much, and getting too much of it can interfere with getting other real goods that one needs, or getting them to the fullest degree in which they are good for us.

There is currently much talk about the sexual revolution—the shift from prohibitive restrictions to almost unlimited permissiveness. This shift is on solid moral grounds, as far as social prohibitions, coercively imposed by the community, are concerned. The community has no grounds whatsoever for prohibiting or censuring simple fornication, or other forms of sexual behavior that were once regarded as perverse or unnatural.

But while the community should be permissive rather than prohibitive, the individual should not be self-indulgently permissive to the extreme at which he becomes a sexual addict. The vicious character of the libertine operates against success in the pursuit of happiness to the same extent and in the same way that the vicious character of the drug addict does, or the alcoholic, the glutton, the money-grubber, or anyone else who has the *bad habit* of seeking a real good to a degree or in a manner that is not good for him or, as in the case of a power-hungry man, the *bad habit* of seeking what is only an apparent good to the displacement or disorder of real goods in his life.

To the question, How much sexual indulgence is compatible with moral virtue?, there is no general answer. It will differ from individual to individual, from one set of external circumstances to another, and for one and the same individual, the answer will differ at different times in his life. To the question, Is this act of fornication good or bad?, there is again no general answer. Rules cannot be formulated to govern such matters. But good habits do govern them.

The man of moral virtue or of good moral character, being one who habitually aims at what is really his own ultimate good, will judge the particular act, not as an isolated singular which, as such, he cannot possibly estimate for its effect on his whole life, but rather as one in a series of acts which, if allowed to occur without limit, would gradually undermine his character and transform him into a vicious man—one who tends habitually away from rather than toward his own ultimate good. In short, it is never a single act of fornication that is to be morally condemned, but rather the habitual fornicator who is disposed to seek sexual pleasure on all occasions and without limit, thus displacing other real goods in the economy of his time and energies.

Note 3. Individual and Common Goods

Real goods are common goods, common in the sense that they are the same for all men because they answer to natural needs, needs inherent in the common or specific nature of man. A good life as a whole is the ultimate common good. The partial goods that constitute this whole or are in some other way means to it are elements or parts of the common good as a whole.

The good of the community is one of these partial goods, and as such it is a means to and element in the ultimate common good. Unlike other real goods that are elements in the ultimate common good, such as health, wealth, pleasure, or knowledge, the good of the community is one that is also common in the special sense of being participated in or shared by the members of a community. Such real goods as health, wealth, pleasure, or knowledge can be possessed and enjoyed by the individual in isolation. They are goods that have their being in the fulfillment of his own natural needs.

In contrast, the good of the community is a good that exists not in the individual as such, but in an organized association of individuals. Nevertheless, it is a good that individual members of the community come to possess and enjoy through their association, and in this sense it is a participated or shared common good. But it must never be thought of as the whole or ultimate common good, for it is only a part or element in the ultimate common good—only a means to the good life for the individual.

I would now like to introduce the phrase "individual goods" to signify the things that an individual wants, whether or not he stands in natural need of them. Individuals differ from one another with respect to their wants or conscious desires, as they do not differ with respect to their needs or natural desires, and it is this fact of individual difference that is being stressed when certain goods are called individual goods rather than common.

What I have just called individual goods are all apparent goods—the things that appear good to the individual or that he calls "good" because he consciously wants them. In a particular instance, the thing that appears good to the individual may also be really good for him because it answers to a natural need. In other words, some of the things men call "good" because they want them are also real goods because they answer to natural needs, but not all apparent goods are also real goods.

In many instances, men want things that are not really good for them, or they want things that are really good, but they want them in a quantity or in a manner that is not really good for them, because the extent or manner in which they want them interferes with their obtaining other real goods that they need. With these considerations in mind, I shall restrict the meaning of the phrase "individual goods," using it to signify only these apparent goods that are *not* really good for the individual, and so are *not* elements in his ultimate common good.

Once these distinctions are understood, the proper order or relation of these various goods becomes immediately evident. It is evident that only the common good that is the whole of all real goods (the *totum bonum commune*) can be the ultimate normative end that is the source of the one primary moral obligation of each individual man—his obligation to make a really good life for himself.

It is evident that all other real goods, being partial goods and elements of the *totum bonum*, must be regarded as means to the one ultimate, normative end that is a good life as a whole. It is evident that the good of the community (*bonum commune communitatis*) is ordered to the ultimate common good of man (*totum bonum commune hominis*) as part to whole, or as means to end.

Finally, it is evident that individual goods (*bonum individuale*)—goods that are not elements in the total common good of the individual, nor indispensable means to his making a good life for himself—can be either detrimental or innocuous. They are innocuous when the individual's effort to obtain these merely apparent goods that he wants does not in any way interfere with or impede his getting the real goods that he needs. They are detrimental when the pursuit of them results in the loss of real goods.

Since the good of the community (*bonum communitatis*) is a real good, an element in the total common good of the individual (*totum bonum commune*), no disorder results when the state requires the individual to sacrifice or to give up individual goods (*bonum individuale*) for the good of the community. On the contrary, the state is then only requiring the individual to give up individual goods that are detrimental to his own ultimate good, since the good of the community is a means to that end.

The same principle of order applies to the individual's private life; his pursuit of individual goods, according to his individual wants, is thoroughly permissible as long as they remain innocuous. However, when they become detrimental, he is morally obligated to desist from their pursuit, for they then become obstacles to, instead of means to, the ultimate end, his good life as a whole, that he is morally obligated to pursue.

Note 4. Moral Obligations to Self and Others

In obeying the injunction to make a good life for himself, it would appear that the individual does not have to take the good of other men into account. The plan for making a good life does not seem to involve any rules or even recommendations concerning the behavior of the individual in relation to other men or to the organized society in which he lives. It may be wondered why the discussion so far has exclusively focused on what is good for the individual, and has totally disregarded his obligation toward others.

This apparent self-centeredness in the development so far of the commonsense view has not been accidental. It springs, in the first place, from the fact that our point of departure was a question with which common sense is concerned and to which commonsense wisdom provides the outlines of an answer—*How can I make a good life for myself?* But that is not the only reason why we have concentrated on what is good for the individual.

The second, and much more important, reason is the commonsense conviction that by the individual's knowing what is really good for himself can he know what is really good for other men, too, and only through knowing this can he determine what an individual's rights are—rights that ought to be secured by society and respected by other men.

Stated in philosophical terms, this commonsense conviction asserts the primacy of the good and the derivative character of the notions of right and wrong. The determination of what is right and wrong in the private or social conduct of the individual is based on what is really good for each individual, and on the *totum bonum* or ultimate end that he ought to seek for himself.

The commonsense view would be seriously defective in its philosophical development if it remained entirely self-centered, but it is not defective by virtue of having made the concern of the individual with his own happiness or good life the point of departure. Quite the contrary. Beginning with self-concern is the only sound approach to the solution of moral problems that involve other men and organized society as well as one's own life. . . .

Resting on the distinction between the real and the apparent good, a basic tenet of the commonsense view is that what is really good for any single individual is good in exactly the same sense for every other human being, precisely because that which is really good is that which satisfies desires or needs inherent in human nature—the makeup that is common to all men because they are members of the same biological species. The *totum bonum*—happiness or the good life—is the same for all men, and each man is under the same basic moral obligation as every other—to make a good life for himself.

Two things follow from this controlling insight. Every real good is a common good, not an individual good, not one that corresponds to the idiosyncratic desires or inclinations of this or that individual. The same, of course, holds true of the *totum bonum* as the sum total of all real goods. The pursuit of happiness by individuals of every shade of individual difference and under every variety of outward circumstance is the pursuit of the same objective.

In addition, when I know the things that are really good for me and what my happiness consists in, and when I understand that each real good and the *totum bonum* as the sum of all of them are common goods, the same for all men, I can then discern the natural rights each individual has—rights that others have which impose moral obligations upon me, and rights that I have which impose moral obligations upon others.

By an individual's rights, we understand the things he has a right to demand of other men or of organized society as a whole. His rights are legal rights when they are granted to him by organized society through the institutions of positive law, including the constitution of the state in which he lives. Conferred upon him by society, they can also be revoked, but while they are in force, each man's legal rights impose legal obligations upon his fellow men.

Where there is no legal right, there is no legal obligation, and conversely, where there is no legal obligation, there is no legal right. The same coimplicative connection exists between moral rights and moral obligations. I can have moral obligations toward another man, and he can have moral obligations toward me, only if each of us has moral rights one against the other.

But what is a moral right as contradistinguished from a legal right? It is obvious at once that it must be a right that exists without being created by positive law or social custom. What is not the product of legal or social conventions must be a creation of nature, or to state the matter more precisely, it must have its being in the nature of men.

Moral rights are natural rights, rights inherent in man's common or specific nature, just as his natural desires or needs are. Such rights, being antecedent to society and government, may be recognized and enforced by society or they may be transgressed and violated, but they are inalienable in the sense that, not being the gift of legal enactment, they cannot be taken away or annulled by acts of government.

The critical point to observe is that natural rights are correlative with natural needs. I said a moment ago that where one individual has an obligation—legal or moral—to another, it must be in virtue of some right—legal or moral—possessed by that other. There is a deeper and more significant connection between rights and obligations, but one that obtains only in the case of moral rights and moral obligations.

I do not have any moral rights vis-à-vis others unless I also have, for each moral right that I claim, a moral obligation to discharge in the sphere of my own private life. Every moral right of mine that imposes a moral duty upon others is inseparable from a moral duty imposed upon me.

For example, if I have a moral—or natural—right to a decent livelihood, that can be the case only because wealth, to a degree that includes amenities as well as bare necessities, is a real good, part of the *totum bonum,* and thus indispensable to a good life. The fact that it is a real good, together with the fact that I am morally obliged to seek it as part of my moral obligation to make a good life for myself, is inseparable from the fact that I have a natural right to a decent livelihood.

If I did not need a modicum of wealth to live well or achieve happiness, it would not be a real good, I would not have a moral obligation to seek it, and *ipso facto* I would also have no natural right to a decent livelihood. That which I do not need for my own good life or that which is not an essential ingredient in my pursuit of happiness does not impose a duty on me, as far as my own private conduct is concerned, nor does it impose a duty on others with regard to their conduct toward me because such matters give me no natural or moral rights that others must respect.

Let me summarize this by calling attention to the set of basic notions that are inseparably connected with one another: (a) natural needs, (b) real goods, (c) the duties or moral obligations I have in the conduct of my own life, (d) moral or natural rights, and (e) the duties or moral obligations I have in my conduct toward others. Natural needs make certain things really good for me; the things that are really good for me impose moral obligations on me in the conduct of my private life; these, in turn, give me certain moral or natural rights, and my having such rights imposes moral obligations on others with respect to me.

The order of enumeration can be reversed, but it cannot be scrambled, and no link in the chain can be omitted. And just as natural needs and the real goods correlative to them are the same for all men because they have the same specific nature, so too, and for the same reason, the remaining items on the list are the same for all men. We all have the same moral obligations in the conduct of our private lives; we all have the same natural rights; and we all have the same duties toward others.

As our primary moral obligation is to make a really good life for ourselves, so our primary natural right is our right to the pursuit of happiness. To respect this right that I have, others are under the obligation not to do anything that prevents me or seriously impedes me from discharging my basic obligation to myself. If I did not know in some detail the things I ought to do in order to discharge the obligation I am under to make a good life for myself, I could not know what behavior on the part of others interfered with my pursuit of happiness and so was wrong—a violation of my natural rights.

In other words, all my subsidiary natural rights—rights to life, security of life and limb, a decent livelihood, freedom from coercion, political liberty, educational opportunities, medical care, sufficient free time for the pursuits of leisure, and so on—stem from my right to the pursuit of happiness and from my obligation to make a good life for myself. They are rights to the things I need to achieve that end and to discharge that obligation. . . .

The individual would not have a natural right to the pursuit of happiness if he did not have a moral obligation to make a good life for himself; and if he did not have that one basic natural right, he would not have any subsidiary natural rights, because all other natural rights relate to the elements of individual happiness or to the parts of a good life—the diverse real goods that, taken together, constitute the whole that is the sum of all these parts.

Note 5. No Conflict Between Self-regarding and Other-regarding Obligations

[What] . . . about the possibility of a conflict between my making a good life for myself and your making one for yourself? . . . I must refer to ideal conditions in order to say that, under such conditions, no possibility of conflict exists.

I injure other men when what I seek for myself deprives them of what they need. Thus, for example, I may seek to exercise power over them in a way that deprives them of the freedom they need to make good lives for themselves. But power or domination over other men is only an apparent good—something I might want, but not something that answers to a natural need. Not being a real good, it is not a means toward making my own life good.

This one example leads us to the insight that when an individual seeks only those things that are really good for him, he does not infringe on or interfere with the pursuit of happiness on the part of others through their seeking the same real goods for themselves. This insight is confirmed by the consideration of the real goods achieved by leisure-work. Nothing that an individual does when engaged in leisure can injure another man; on the contrary, through his engagement in leisure, the individual not only benefits himself but usually benefits others.

Wealth and pleasure are also real goods, but only in limited quantities and only as subordinated to the goods of self-improvement—the goods achieved by leisure. Hence it is possible for an individual to seek wealth or pleasure to an extent or in a manner that is injurious to others. But this can happen only when what he seeks or the way he seeks it is, like power or domination over other men, not really good for him—something he may want, and so something that is an apparent good, but not something that answers to a natural need, and so not something that is really good.

If what I have just said were not so, two things would follow. My seeking the things that are really good for me would lead me to infringe on the rights of others—their rights to the things that are really good for them. It would then be impossible to say that the pursuit of happiness is the basic natural right a government must attempt to secure for every individual, if it is to be a just government, for if some men's pursuit of happiness required them to impede or frustrate others in the exercise of the same right, no government could discharge its obligation to be just to all its subjects. . . .

I come, finally, to the problem of how my being just toward others, under ideal conditions that make such conduct on my part possible, promotes my own pursuit of happiness—in short, how justice toward others is an integral part of my making a good life for myself. The solution of this problem is contained to some extent in the solutions to the other two related problems we have just considered. On the one hand, there is the positive point that justice toward others is a means to the civil peace of the community, and that—the essential good of the community—is in turn a means that serves me in making a good life for myself.

On the other hand, there is the negative point that under ideal conditions, my seeking the things that are really good for me does not require me to injure anyone else. It is only when I seek goods that I may want but do not need, that I may be led, even under ideal conditions, to deprive others of the things they need; and so I may be led to violate their natural rights.

The negative point just made can be given a positive rendering and one that enhances its significance. We have seen that moral virtue, in the aspect of fortitude or of temperance, disposes a man to choose between alternatives in such a way that his choice of this rather than that is for the sake of making a good life for himself. The virtuous man, in short, is not only one who has this end in view, but also one who is disposed to choose, from day to day, what is really good for himself in the long run, as against what is only apparently good here and now.

But it is only when a man is disposed to prefer apparent goods to real goods that he is also inclined to gratify wants or to gratify them in such a way that he injures others by depriving them of what they need for a good life. Hence the man who, in the conduct of his private affairs, lacks fortitude and temperance is also one who will be unjust in his conduct toward others, and for the very reason that he is not well disposed in the conduct of his own life.

The other face of the same truth is that the man who is inclined to be unjust toward others can be so only through lack of virtue in the conduct of his own life, whereby he is disposed to prefer apparent to real goods for himself. This amounts to saying that the good moral character a man must have in order to make a good life for himself is identical with the good moral character he must have in order to act justly toward others.

When a man's moral virtue operates in the sphere of his private affairs, temperance and fortitude are the appropriate names for the aspects of his good character. When his virtue operates in relation to the rights of others or the good of the community, justice is the appropriate name for the aspect of good character involved. But since, in any of its aspects, virtue consists in being disposed to choose real as against apparent goods, justice toward others is existentially inseparable from fortitude and temperance. It is analytically distinct from them only in its relational aspect— its relation to the good of others.

Since a good moral character is a necessary means toward making a good life for oneself, it follows that justice toward others is also a means to the same end, for justice is nothing but a good moral character operating in relation to the rights of others and the good of the community.

I think it is now clear how the individual's pursuit of happiness, how his effort to make a good life for himself, is related to the rights of others and to the good of the organized community. But in making this clear, I have repeatedly qualified what I have said by referring to *ideal conditions*. The significance of that qualification must now be explained.

By "ideal" I do not mean a state of affairs that is perfect in every way. That is utopian and unattainable. I mean no more than normal or healthy. Thus, if the purpose of men in associating is to enjoy the good of communal life, which is peace, then war in any form represents a pathological social condition, one that defeats the very purpose for which men associate.

A society rent by civil strife or one that is engaged in external war is malfunctioning, and in the medical sense of the term, it is pathological or abnormal. If I speak of war as an instance of social pathology or abnormality in this sense, I am obviously not using the word "abnormal" to mean *unusual in a statistical sense*, since either through civil strife or external conflicts, almost all societies from the beginning of history have been abnormal or pathological.

Another example may help to reinforce what I have just said. The purpose of men in associating in families or in states is not only to enjoy the blessings of peace, but also to achieve other goods that the isolated individual could not achieve for himself. Among these are wealth, a decent supply of the means of subsistence, and sufficient free time for the goods that can be achieved through play and leisure. So when the technological conditions of a society are such that widespread poverty or destitution cannot be eliminated, and the lives of most men are consumed in backbreaking toil from dawn to dusk, working in a state of chattel slavery or abject servitude, the society is pathological or abnormal in the sense indicated. It is not functioning as a society should; that is, it is not serving the purpose for which men form associations. Once again it must be said that from the beginning of history to the present time, most, if not all, societies have been pathological or abnormal.

When I use the word "ideal" to signify the opposite of pathological or abnormal, I am expressing the conviction that the pathological conditions so far mentioned are remediable or curable. We have reached that point in the historical development of man's life on earth where we can at last begin to see how war, poverty, and slavery or servitude can be eliminated.

Therefore, by "ideal conditions" I mean no more than a state of society in which all eliminable evils have been eliminated. The amount of crime can be reduced, but it is highly doubtful that crime can ever be totally eliminated. I would not include the elimination of crime as an element in what I mean by ideal conditions.

How does social pathology, or the absence of ideal conditions, affect the problems with which we are concerned?

In the first place, the conditions of social life may be such that no man can succeed in making a good life for himself; or, when the pathology is less extreme, the opportunity of making a good life may be open only to the few. In the latter case, the fewer still who make use of that opportunity and do succeed in making good lives for themselves will necessarily have done so at the expense of misery for the many who are deprived. I say "necessarily" to indicate that it may have been impossible at the time, the state of technology being what it was, to provide sufficient free time or a decent supply of the means of subsistence for more than the few. . . .

Neither individuals nor governments are guilty of injustice when the conditions are such that it is impossible to secure for all their natural rights. It is only under ideal conditions which make doing justice possible, that an individual or a government is morally condemnable for failing to act justly.

That is why I said earlier that it is only under ideal conditions that an individual can make a good life for himself without injuring anyone else in the course of doing so; more than that, under such conditions, he will not succeed in making a good life for himself if his character is such that he is disposed to injure others in the course of seeking what he wants in preference to what he needs.

The social pathology that is war, especially war between states, has a different effect. We have seen that the good of the community is a means to the ultimate end of each of its individual members; namely, the good life or happiness of each. To subordinate the individual's ultimate good to the good of the state is to pervert this order of goods by converting what is only a means into an ultimate end. Yet when the state is at war with other states, individuals are called upon to take risks or to use their time in such a way that their success in making good lives for themselves is seriously jeopardized or at least impeded to an extent.

What is true of the pathological condition that is external war is also true when civil strife breaks out, and when natural disasters, such as earthquakes and floods, famines and pestilences, occur. In all these cases, individuals are called upon to act for the good of the community, sometimes even for its survival, in a way that either jeopardizes their success in the pursuit of happiness or at least seriously impedes their efforts. Nevertheless, none of these instances of social pathology, not even the most extreme, should lead us to the false conclusion that the good of the community is the ultimate good in which resides the primary moral obligation of men.

Even under the most extreme pathological conditions, the state cannot rightly ask the individual totally to sacrifice his life, or his pursuit of happiness, for its own good, or its survival. It can rightly ask the individual to do no more than take risks or suffer temporary inconveniences. To understand this is to understand that, under ideal conditions, the individual who acts for the good of the community is acting wholly and in every way for his own ultimate good. Under such conditions, nothing he does for the good of the community either jeopardizes or impedes his efforts to make a good life for himself.

Note 6. The Difference Between Risk and Sacrifice

Let me first quote Monsignor John Ryan on the point. "It is not reasonable to expect men to devote themselves to any other end than their own highest [more precisely, complete] good, and a superior society cannot be the highest good for those who must be annihilated as a condition of its realization. They will very naturally prefer to run the risk of securing their own welfare in a less perfect social organization. There is no duty constraining one section of the community—not simply to risk their lives, as in a just war—but to submit to be killed by the social authority, in order that the surviving citizens may have the benefit of a more efficient state" (John A. Ryan, *A Living Wage*, pp. 55–56).

The essential point here is the difference between risk and sacrifice. Under pathological social conditions, such as war or any other dire emergency, the individual may either volunteer to do things that involve serious threats to his pursuit of a good life for himself, or he may be required by the state to take such risks. But in no case can he be asked to lay down his life for his country, for that would involve a profound perversion in the order of goods—the subordination of the *totum bonum hominis,* which is the ultimate end, to one of its means, the *bonum communitatis.*

Nevertheless, there seem to be circumstances in which the state does ask men to jeopardize their health and even their lives for the good of the community. If this demand is just—and let us concede that it sometimes may be—then it would *appear* that the good of the community (*bonum communitatis*) takes precedence over happiness (*totum bonum hominis*), for if a man endangers his health and risks his life for the good of the community, he would seem to be forgoing the pursuit of happiness, which requires health and certainly life. It is only by considering dire emergencies that we can see how asking men to take certain risks can be justified, since the long-term consequences of their not taking risks may be even more detrimental to their achievement of happiness than putting themselves in temporary jeopardy.

During a serious epidemic, which endangers the state's well-being by threatening to decimate its population, all men, not only physicians and nurses, can be impressed into the service of public health, even at the risk of their own health, and perhaps life. When a community is similarly threatened by earthquake or flood, all of its members can be similarly expected to assume perilous risks.

In times of peace, not only are officers charged with enforcing the law duty-bound to risk their lives in the apprehension of criminals, but so, in fact, is every citizen obligated to assist the police, if there be such need, or even, in the absence of police, to undertake the dangerous task of blocking the path of dangerous criminals. This case is misunderstood if it is supposed that the duty here lies between one individual and another, the one risking his health or life to protect the life or property of another. The obligation in justice is rather a civic duty to protect the peace and order of the community against the ravages of crime. The public peace of a community is as much menaced, though seldom as dramatically, by the spread of unchecked crime within its borders as by the advance of unchecked aggressors upon its territorial domains.

Hence the duty of a citizen in time of peace is no different from his duty in time of war, though under the conditions of modern warfare, which efface the ancient distinction between soldiers and noncombatants, every member of the community is more likely to experience the precariousness of a front line position in defense of the community's existence.

The emergency of war differs from the emergency of crime in one other respect; not only is it usually a more intense emergency, having a more widespread impact on the whole population simultaneously, but it raises a question of justice which crime by definition does not. Absolutely speaking, no citizen can be justly required to take part in a purely predatory, or unjust, attack upon another community. The use of military force against outsiders is justified only in defense, just as the use of police power within the state is justified only by crime.

With all this understood, we must still ask, How can justice require us to risk our lives, or anything essential to happiness, such as health, even in those emergencies in which the state's survival or its peace is threatened? The answer turns on the fact that what is required is only a *risk*, and not an *absolute surrender*, of these essential goods. *The risk of life is not suicide.* Regardless of how dire the emergency may be, the state cannot ask a man to kill himself for its good. Nor can the state kill men who have not forfeited their lives by criminal attack upon the social welfare.

Whether or not the capital punishment of criminals is justified by retributive justice, it is certainly true that apart from the sort of violence through which a man declares himself to be an enemy of the state, the state cannot kill men without committing the injustice of murder. Suppose a famine or a pestilence and suppose it would be obviously expedient, in the protection of the whole community, to kill a few—the aged or the infected. Is it not perfectly obvious that such expedients cannot be resorted to because they violate justice? And they violate justice because they wrongly place the good of the community before and above the inalienable rights of each individual to life, liberty, and the pursuit of happiness.

Though it deprives men of less than life, the sterilization of the unfit is also judged to be contrary to justice, regardless of how strong a case can be made out, on clear factual grounds, for its expedience. Now, if the *bonum communitatis* were the *totum bonum*, if within the sphere of means and ends the *bonum communitatis* were the ultimate end, whatever was *truly expedient* as a means to it would be *naturally justified*.

These things not being so, we return to the important distinction between the *probablity of risk* and the *certainty of sacrifice*. And the probablity of risk is related to another probablity—the *probability of threatening ruin* which confronts the state in dire civic emergencies. If it were possible to know with certitude that despite all efforts, the state was doomed to perish in this emergency, there would be no point to risking one's life, nor could that risk be justly required; just as, if it were possible to know with certitude that the act one was about to perform for the state's defense would lead to death, the act could not be obligated or rendered in justice for it would be murder (by the state which demanded it) or suicide (by the individual who, believing himself bound in justice, rendered it).

To stay within the bounds of justice, we must stay within the domain of probabilities, in which there is a proportionality between the probable risk the individual undertakes and the probable threat the state faces. Within this domain we can understand why the state can ask, and why the individual can render, a service that *appears* to violate the order of real goods. The violation is only apparent because the risk the individual takes is balanced against another probability which threatens him. If the state were to perish, the individual himself might not survive the catastrophe, or at least its consequence would be a drastic impairment of the conditions he needed for continuing his pursuit of happiness. Therefore, he risks his life in the hope, not only of his own survival, but of the community's preservation and future prosperity, so that, the emergency surmounted, the danger past, peace and safety once more regained, the state will continue to play its normal role as a common good to be enjoyed and as a means to be used.

Within the sphere of probabilities, which permit men to cherish hope in the face of risks and threats, the individual does not *naturally* hope for the state's safety with no concern for his own fate, nor does he hope for his own survival with no thought of his community's endurance; rather he hopes that good fortune will attend his efforts in respect to both goods, and he hopes for both because either without the other would frustrate the intentions of his natural appetite.

Moreover, the order of his hopes follows the order of his intentions; as both self-preservation and a benevolent society are means necessitated by happiness as the end, so does he hope for his own survival and the state's endurance as indispensable conditions prerequisite to the attainment of happiness. These two goods are not only means to the same end, but reciprocally means to each other, though not with the same stress under conditions of safety and peril; whereas under circumstances of peace and security society provides its members with aid in the struggle for subsistence, the reverse causality predominates in times of war and impending disaster, when men must help the state survive.

Because these two means to happiness (individual subsistence and society's endurance) are thus coimplicated in reciprocal causality, because the emergency situation involves two inseparable risks, not one, the individual is not free to disregard one threat and protect himself entirely against the other. His individual happiness is doubly threatened by the emergency; it is as much threatened by the probability that the community will not endure unless its members will assume risks proportionate to this danger, as it is threatened by the probability that he may perish if he undertakes to prevent disaster to the community.

Clearly, then, it follows that when a man acts in such situations with the fortitude that justice commands, he is not exalting the good of the community above his individual happiness, and when the state justly exacts such conduct from its members, it is not preferring its own life to the life of its members, but rather regarding both as means to happiness and both as inseparably threatened.

Each member of the community enjoys the *bonum communitatis*, and profits by the state's ministry to his individual welfare. Each individual must, therefore, be prepared to pay a price, in effort and risk, for these benefits, because he cannot avoid such effort and risk without risking their total loss. But since, in a just community, all share equally in the *bonum communitatis* and all profit proportionately from its benefactions, the principle of justice requires a fair distribution of burdens to balance the distributive justice of properly shared goods.

It is this principle which completes our resolution of the apparent conflict between the good of the community and the happiness of its members. If the burdens of effort and risk are justly distributed among the members of a community, each is called upon to do no more than the rest in the protection and support of goods they commonly enjoy and proportionately share. No man would then be sacrificing himself in any way for his fellows. Justice, be it remembered, never calls for sacrifice or generosity; it exacts only a just price; it asks only for what is due.

Accordingly, if distributive justice prevails with respect to common goods and common burdens alike, then each man who acts justly in the performance of his civic duty in times of emergency cooperates with his fellows for the social welfare so that it in turn will continue to support the welfare of himself. Each acts with all for the good of all because upon that depends the good of each. And no risk of life can be too great so long as it is proportionate in its probability to the probability of disaster which threatens the state, and so long as one man's assumption of risk is not proportionately greater than another's.

If it were possible, in a complex modern society, for each man to think that everyone else was bearing proportionate burdens and risks—as that is almost certainly known by the members of a small frontier community—then justice would be sufficient; the just man would not hesitate to face the greater risks for the community's welfare. But since in any large and complex society, the ideal of distributive justice is very imperfectly realized, and individuals are beset by doubts about the full cooperation of their fellow men in a common cause, justice is not enough to impel men to take the risk which may turn out, in fact, to have been a sacrifice, because it exceeded the risks others have assumed. In such a situation, love is required. Only through love for one's fellow man is anyone impelled, beyond mere justice, to take the chance of doing more than others. And it is certainly a question of whether ordinary human love is enough.

It is of the utmost importance to distinguish between the sacrifice of individual goods for the sake of the general welfare, which the state can justly require of its citizens, and the sacrifice of the individual's pursuit of happiness for the good of the community, which the state can never justly demand. Individual goods, by definition, are not common goods—not elements in the *totum bonum*. Hence sacrificing them, even when they are innocuous, does not interfere with the pursuit of happiness. Not being either real goods or common goods, individual goods cannot be claimed as a matter of natural right. Depriving the individual of them is, therefore, not an act of injustice.

Let us, for the moment, consider only such individual goods as are innocuous, and are not subject to the prohibition that they ought not to be sought by the individual for the sake of his own happiness. Such individual goods, being only apparent goods, are subordinate in the scale of values to real and common goods, the *bonum commune communitatis* as well as the *totum bonum commune hominis*. As subordinate, they should be sought or possessed only on condition that they remain innocuous, i.e., on condition that they do not interfere with or impede the attainment of any real good by the individual himself or by his fellow men.

When the state justly calls for the sacrifice of individual goods on the part of its members, it does so either on the grounds that the good of the community itself is thereby served, or on the grounds that the sacrifice serves the general welfare. The state, as we shall see presently, has a double obligation in justice to its citizens, the *negative* obligation not to deprive them of the things to which they have a natural right, and the *positive* obligation to help them obtain the things they need for the pursuit of happiness. In discharging this positive obligation, the state promotes the general welfare, in which, under a just constitution and just laws, all citizens share equally.

Therefore, we should be able to see that when the state requires its citizens to sacrifice individual goods either for the sake of the good of the community or in order to promote the general welfare, that sacrifice on the part of individuals is for their own ultimate good, since the *bonum communitatis* is a part of the *totum bonum hominis* and since the promotion of the general welfare is a means to that same end.

Failure to understand this has led men to the violent extremes of either individualism or totalitarianism, and the resultant controversy is made bitter by the fact that each extreme holds on to a half-truth which it cannot, and should not, surrender, but which it must not exaggerate into the whole truth at the expense of denying the complementary part.

That, of course, is precisely what happens when the totalitarian, rightly demanding the sacrifice of individual goods for the good of the community and the general welfare, denies that individual happiness matters at all, and when the individualist, on his side, rightly affirms that the ultimate good is the happiness of the individual, but fails to understand happiness as a common good, and so regards any encroachment of the state on the propensities of the individual as an evil.

The truth that man is not made for the state, but the state for man, means that man makes the state for his own ultimate good. He cannot, therefore, reasonably object to whatever is justly required by the state in order for it to serve effectively the purpose for which it was made.

Note 7. David Hume on the Fallacy of Inferring Prescriptive from Descriptive Statements

Hume's statement reads as follows: "I cannot forbear adding to these reasonings an observation, which may, perhaps, be found of some importance. In every system of morality which I have hitherto met with, I have always remarked, that the author proceeds for some time in the ordinary way of reasoning, and establishes the being of a God, or makes observations concerning human affairs; when of a sudden I am surprised to find, that instead of the usual copulations of propositions, *is* and *is not*, I meet with no proposition that is not connected with an *ought* or an *ought not*. This change is imperceptible; but is, however, of the last consequence. For as this *ought*, or *ought not*, expresses some new relation or affirmation, it is necessary that it should be observed and explained; and at the same time that a reason should be given, for what seems altogether inconceivable, how this new relation can be a deduction from others, which are entire different from it. But as authors do not commonly use this precaution, I shall presume to recommend it to the readers; and am persuaded, that this small attention would subvert all the vulgar systems of morality. . . ."[1]

Note 8. Criticism of Roman Stoicism

The ethics of the Roman Stoics is self-refuting. If the individual cannot be injured, as the Stoics claim, by anything he suffers at

---

[1] David Hume, *A Treatise of Human Nature*, Book III, Part I, Section I.

the hands of fortune or of other men, then there are no grounds for saying, as the Stoics maintain, that the individual's only good lies in the goodness of his own will, a goodness the individual is said to possess when he does his duty toward society and acts rightly toward other men.

If the individual cannot injure others, because no individual can be injured by another, how, then, can the virtuous man of good will, who does his duty and acts rightly, be distinguished from the vicious man who has injured himself alone by the badness of his own will?

If one man cannot injure another, injustice is impossible, and if injustice is impossible, how can a man's will be good or bad, and his actions right or wrong, in relation to others?

Conversely, if justice is possible, and if one man can injure another in various ways, but never by destroying the goodness of that other man's will, then the total good of each individual must include more than goodness of his own will, and that *totum bonum* must be the basis of determining what is right and wrong in the conduct of one individual toward another.

Note 9. Critique of Immanuel Kant's Moral Philosophy

In my judgment, the single most important contribution made by Kant to the formation of moral philosophy was his insistence that it should be able validly to formulate categorical obligations universally binding on all men in the same way. Any ethical doctrine or theory of human character and conduct that falls short of this may contain pragmatic or utilitarian wisdom; it may set forth reasonable and empirically sound recommendations about how men should act if they wish to achieve certain ends; it may even express generally agreed upon appreciations of the relative value of one end as against another, and cultivate attitudes of respect for and devotion to ideals that are noble and honorable; but if its fundamental principles do not include categorical obligations universally binding on all men in the same way, then, however sound or wise it may be in other respects, it does not have the soundness or wisdom of moral philosophy. The ethics of common sense . . . meets Kants requirement.

* * *

There is one passage in Kant's writings that appears to agree with the thesis that the individual's moral obligation to himself takes precedence over his duties toward others and is, in a sense, their root. He writes: "No one has framed a proper concept of self-regarding duty. It has been treated as a detail and considered by way of an afterthought, as an appendix to moral philosophy, on the view that man should give thought to himself only after he has completely fulfilled his duty toward others. All moral philosophies err in this respect. . . . Far from ranking lowest in the scale of precedence, our duties toward ourselves are of primary importance and should have pride of place . . . the prior condition of our duty toward others is our duty to ourselves; we can fulfill the former only insofar as we must first fulfill the latter."

However, the appearance of agreement between the Kantian position and that of the commonsense view is completely dispelled by the following statements that occur within the context of the passage quoted above. "It was taken for granted that a man's duty toward himself consisted, as Wolff in his turn defined it, in promoting his own happiness. In that case, everything would depend on how an individual determined his own happiness. [Note here Kant's assumption of the relativity of the individual's happiness to his own individual wants, without any regard for the distinction between real and apparent goods. What Kant says in the very next sentence follows as a consequence of this mistaken conception of happiness.] This would, however, militate seriously against doing our duty toward others. In fact, the principle of self-regarding duties is a very different one, *which has no connexion with our well-being or earthly happiness*" (italics added). [2]

Kant is correct in thinking that the individual's primary devotion to his own happiness, *if that were relative to his individual wants*, would militate against his doing his duty toward others. But that, as we have seen, is an incorrect—a psychological and nonmoral—conception of happiness.

When happiness is conceived, in moral terms, as identical with

[2] Immanuel Kant, *Lectures on Ethics*, pp. 177–178.

a whole life that is really good, Kant's insistence on the primacy of self-concern and his insight that the individual's duties toward others are subordinate to his primary obligation to himself, are more significantly and consistently carried out in the commonsense view, which makes happiness or the *totum bonum* the ultimate end and the primary object of obligation, than they are in Kantian ethics, which makes the individual's only duty to himself a duty to perfect his will by conforming it to the moral law. ... The ethics of common sense resembles the ethics of Kant in certain purely formal respects, but they differ radically on all essential points of substance.

The fundamental flaw here lies in Kant's misconception of happiness as the satisfaction of individual wants or inclinations, which makes it impossible for him to avoid an ambiguous use of the term "happiness" when he speaks of the virtuous man being worthy of happiness, as the vicious man is not. This does not preclude the vicious man from achieving happiness, in his own terms; nor does it guarantee that the virtuous man who is worthy of happiness will attain it.

In addition, Kant misconceives virtue as a good in itself, the only thing—a virtuous or good will—that is good without qualification. In this respect, his position resembles that of the ancient Stoics and is subject to the same difficulties. Far from being good without qualification, moral virtue or a virtuous will is only an instrumental means to happiness, and its goodness is that of a means, not an end, and only that of an instrumental means, not a constitutive means—not a real good that is part of happiness, but a causal factor indispensable in the pursuit of it.

Kant's solution of the problems with which we have been concerned is unsatisfactory for other reasons. We saw earlier the indefensibility of Kant's position with respect to what he calls "ethical duties"—duties attached to ends. It is also indefensible with respect to what he calls "legal duties"—the duties that are discharged by obedience to the moral law. These duties, such as the duty to keep promises, the duty to pay debts, the duty to tell the truth, are neither self-evident in themselves, as later deontologists incorrectly suppose, nor can they be logically derived from the categorical imperative, as Kant's sharpest critics have pointed out again and again. Since they are not self-evident, some reason must be given for regarding them as obligations that govern our conduct toward our fellow men.

The only reason that can be given must involve a reference, first, to the possibility that my telling another man a lie, my refusing to pay him back what I owe him, or my failing to keep my promise to him, may injure him, that is, may prevent or impede his making a good life for himself, and second, it must also involve some assessment of the probablity that such is the case.

The question of probability is one of fact; the possibility under consideration can be established only by thinking, first, in terms of what is really good and bad for the other man in order to decide; second, what may be right or wrong for me to do in relation to him. On both counts—the primacy of the good over the right and the appeal to empirical facts—we have had to depart radically from Kant's scheme of things in order to give any defense, however weak, of the moral obligations he regards as legal duties.

The harshness of Kant's moral philosophy has made it generally repugnant to men who do not confuse being reasonable with being rationalistic. It demands of us, in the sphere of legal obligations, that we do our duty simply and purely for duty's sake and without any regard for our natural inclinations or needs, or concern for our own happiness. It calls upon us, in the sphere of ethical obligations, to act for the happiness of others but not our own. And in both spheres, it proceeds without any reference to the facts of human nature and human behavior, and rules out any consideration of such facts—or, for that matter, of particular circumstances—as irrelevant to the determination of what is good and bad, right and wrong.

Nevertheless, one might be reluctantly driven to accept Kant's harsh and arid ethics if the only alternative to it were what he calls "the serpentine windings of utilitarianism"; then our only choice would be between a moral philosophy that has autonomy, on the one hand, and purely pragmatic doctrine, on the other.

Fortunately, we are not confronted with the choice; the ethics of common sense involves the cautionary consideration of circumstances, the pragmatic calculation of the utility of means, and the regard for individual differences which are to be found in utilitarianism, while at the same time it is a moral philosophy that has autonomous principles and normative truths capable of unrestricted universalization.

It may be objected that the ethics of Kant is not a purely deontological ethics; it may be claimed by Kantians that it is also teleological, for it treats of ends that are duties and is concerned with the problem of ultimate ends.

Two things plainly reveal that Kant's ethics is not teleological: (a) though he treats of ends, he never considers the means for achieving them, and to discuss ends without reference to means is empty talk; (b) his rationalistic purity prevents him from dealing with means, for it is impossible to consider means in relation to ends without reference to empirical knowledge of matters of fact, and Kant excludes such considerations from moral philosophy as the product of pure practical reason.

In consequence, his ethics cannot be either teleological or practical, and even in those passages in which Kant *appears* to be thinking teleologically, he fails to make the happiness that he acknowledges to be man's ultimate end the primary object of his moral obligation, and the source of all other derivative duties; in short, he fails to subordinate the right to the good, and the deontological formulation of categorical oughts to the teleological consideration of the *totum bonum commune* and the means of achieving it.

The ethics of common sense accepts as thoroughly correct Kant's criticism of all the merely empirical, pragmatic, or utilitarian substitutes for moral philosophy, which proceed solely in terms of means and ends and wholly by reference to matters of fact, without acknowledging a single categorical ought. In the absence of categorical oughts, thinking about the problems of action may be practical or pragmatic, but its conclusions lack the character of moral judgments.

On the other hand, by thinking in terms of categorical oughts, as well as in terms of end and means (the latter on the basis of factual knowledge), teleological ethics is a moral philosophy that is also empirical and pragmatic—the only form of moral philosophy that is.

In contrast, the deontological ethics of Kant or of his followers is, by the self-limitations it insists on—the exclusion of all reference to matters of fact as bearing on means and ends—a moral philosophy that is neither empirical nor practical. It is rationalistic or *a priori* and purely formal to an absurd extreme. It is offered as a product of *pure practical reason* which, precisely because it tries to be *pure*, ceases to be *practical*.

Confronted with the prescriptions of a purely deontological ethics, out of all touch with the facts of life, any man of common sense would know at once that it is of little or no practical guidance to him in solving the problems of life or action, especially the central and controlling problem of a good life for himself and right action toward others.

Here is the mistake made by Kant in his criticism of any moral philosophy that regards happiness as the *summum bonum*—the highest or supreme good—and proceeds by prescribing the means to be employed or the courses of action to be followed in order to achieve happiness as the ultimate end or goal of human activity. Such prescriptions, according to Kant, take the form of hypothetical, not categorical, oughts. Even though, as a matter of fact, all men may want happiness, the recommendations for achieving it are purely pragmatic or utilitarian, and lack the quality of moral rules, because they are concerned exclusively with means to an end that *is* desired, not one that *ought* to be desired.

In Kant's view, the only end or good the individual ought to desire for himself is his own moral perfection—the perfection of his will—and this means that he ought to desire, not happiness, but being morally worthy of happiness. The *summum bonum*, in the sense of the highest good, is the moral perfection of a good will, but if the *summum bonum* is interpreted to mean not the *highest* good, but the *complete* good, then it consists in the combination of being happy with the state of being worthy of happiness through the attainment of moral perfection.

Before I point out how Kant's failure to recognize the distinction between the real and the apparent good vitiates his argument, I would like to show why Kant's argument appears to challenge the soundness of the commonsense view that one ought to make a good life for oneself. His analysis of duties or obligations leads him from the consideration of legal duties that can be enforced by external sanctions to the consideration of ethical duties that cannot be so enforced. Kant describes these duties as "Ends which are also Duties"; that is, they are goods that impose moral obligations upon us: we *ought* to seek or promote them. They divide into one's duty to oneself and one's duty to others.

The former consists exclusively in one's obligation to seek one's own moral perfection by willing and acting in conformity with the moral law. The latter consists, also exclusively, in one's obligation to promote the happiness of others. In expounding these two basic ethical duties, Kant explicitly denies, on the one hand, the existence or even the possibility of an obligation on the individual's part to seek his own happiness; as, on the other hand, he just as explicitly denies the existence of even the possibility of the individual's having a duty to act for or promote the moral perfection of others.

To give the foregoing analysis the appearance of relevance to the commonsense view being developed, let us for the moment suppose that what Kant means by happiness is identical with the conception of a good life. If that were the case, then Kant would have to be interpreted as maintaining that the individual is under no obligation to make a good life for himself, though he is under an obligation to do what he can to promote a good life for others. The commonsense view that each of us ought to make a good life for himself would have to be rejected.

Commenting on "the conception of the '*Summum Bonum*,'" Kant observes that "the conception of the *summum* itself contains an ambiguity which might occasion needless disputes, if we did not attend to it. The *summum* may mean either the supreme (*supremum*) or the perfect (*consummatum*)"[3]

In spite of this observation, Kant continually makes use of this highly ambiguous epithet. It seems to me mandatory to replace it by the phrase *totum bonum* when what is meant is not one good of supreme value as distinguished from other and inferior goods, but rather the whole or sum total of all real goods, however they may be ordered as inferior and superior from lowest to highest.

Kant's playing with the ambiguity of "*summum bonum*" is matched by his playing with the ambiguity of "happiness." He uses it, on the one hand, to signify the satisfaction of the individual's desires whatever they may be and, on the other hand, to signify only the satisfaction of virtuous desires on the part of the man whose attainment of happiness is deserved. All these ambiguities are multiplied in the following passage: "Happiness alone is, in the view of reason, far from being the complete good. Reason does not approve of it (however much inclination may desire it), except as united with desert. On the other hand, morality alone, and with it mere desert, is likewise far from being the complete good. To make it complete, he who conducts himself in a manner not unworthy of happiness must be able to hope, for the possession of happiness. . . . Happiness, therefore, in exact proportion with the morality of rational beings (whereby they are made worthy of happiness), constitues alone the supreme good of a world in which we absolutely must transport ourselves according to the commands of pure but practical reason."[4]

If Kant had used the term "happiness" as a purely ethical term, synonymous with a good life as the *totum bonum* (the sum total of the goods that all men ought to want and that morally virtuous men do want), he would have seen that happiness is *unattainable by men who, lacking virtue, are also unworthy of it,* and he might also have realized that virtuous men, who deserve happiness, can be prevented by misfortunes beyond their control from achieving it.

If we were to make this one correction in Kant's thought, and,

[3] Immanuel Kant, *Critique of Practical Reason, p. 206.*
[4] Kant, *Critique of Pure Reason,* p. 457.

together with all that it implies, were to follow it through relentlessly, we would erode most of what is distinctive about Kant's moral philosophy, including all it rationalistic purity and its formalistic trappings. The appeal to pure reason and the specious process of deducing specific duties from the categorical imperative would be replaced by a determination of particular obligations with respect to real goods that ought to be sought on the basis of the empirically known facts of human nature and human behavior.

The development of moral philosophy in the last 150 years might have taken a radically different course if Kant had not misconceived happiness and had not ignored human nature as the source of our knowledge of what is ultimately good for man, which in turn is the basis of our categorical obligations with regard to the various means to this end.

In the full development of the commonsense view, the obligation of the individual to make a good life for himself is not only a valid categorical ought, but it is the one primary obligation from which all other obligations and duties, whether to self or to others, can be derived. The ethics of common sense will be seen to resemble the moral philosophy of Kant only in the formal respect that both attempt to combine the teleological consideration of ends that are good with the deontological formulation of categorical oughts; but on all major points of substance within that framework, the ethics of common sense and the moral philosophy of Kant are diametrically opposed.

Note 10. John Stuart Mill's Utilitarianism and Immanuel Kant's Rationalism

Though the ethics of common sense is both teleological and deontological, it is primarily teleological because the *totum bonum* as ultimate end is its first principle and the object of the one basic moral obligation—the obligation to make a life that is really good as a whole. Every other good is a means to this end; every other moral obligation, either in regard to the goods one ought to seek for oneself or in regard to rights of others, derives from the one basic moral obligation that relates to the ultimate normative end of all our actions.

In order to be both teleological and deontological, and, more than that, in order properly to subordinate the deontological to the teleological, deriving categorical oughts from the consideration of end and means, an ethics must (a) affirm the primacy of the good and (b) distinguish between real and apparent goods.

That is why the ethics of Kant and of Mill only *appear* to be both, but under careful scrutiny are not. While Kant appears to be concerned with ends as well as duties, he makes duties—or the right, not the good—primary. And while Mill appears to be concerned with duties as well as with ends and means, his failure to recognize the distinction between real and apparent goods prevents him from making ends and means objects of categorical obligation.

It would be impossible for organized society to do justice by securing, both positively and negatively, the fundamental right of all its members—the right to the pursuit of happiness—unless happiness were a common good, a *totum bonum* that is the same for all men. Let it be, as Kant and Mill conceive it, nothing but the satisfaction of conscious desires, whatever they may be, without regard to the distinction between real and apparent goods; the variety of goals that men would then pursue in the name of happiness, many of them bringing individuals into serious conflict with one another, could not constitute all together the common objective of a government's efforts to promote the general welfare. It would be under conflicting obligations that it could not discharge.

Only if happiness is the same for all men, and involves them in the pursuit of real goods that are common goods, does the pursuit of happiness not bring individuals into conflict with one another, and make it possible for a government to secure, equally, for each and every one of them, their natural rights.

Note 11. Critique of John Stuart Mill's Utilitarianism

The main trouble with utilitarianism is not the principle of utility itself, for that must govern any moral thinking that is done in terms of ends and means. Any teleological ethics, such as that of common sense, is utilitarian or pragmatic in its employment of the principle of utility in appraising the goodness of means. The trouble with utilitarianism is that it is a teleological ethics with not one but two ultimate ends, and the two cannot be reconciled to each other or fused into a single overarching goal that can be the object of one primary moral obligation.

By consulting the actual desires of men, Mill concludes that everyone seeks his own happiness. Let us waive for the moment the error of identifying the happiness made up of the things an individual happens to want with the happiness constituted by the real and common goods every man ought to seek. Still using happiness to signify the sum total of satisfactions experienced by the individual who gets whatever he wants for himself, Mill then tries to substitute the general happiness or the greatest good of the greatest number for individual happiness as the ultimate goal.

Having first said, as a matter of fact, that each man desires his own happiness, conceived by him in terms of his own wants, Mill then shifts to saying that the ultimate standard or objective, in accordance with which the principle of utility should be applied, is "not the agent's own greatest happiness, but the greatest amount of happiness altogether."

With regard to the individual's own happiness, Mill sees no need to argue for it as the ultimate end, since in fact all men do desire it. But when he comes to the "general happiness," Mill finds it impossible to say that, as a matter of fact, everyone desires this as his ultimate end. He considers the man who says to himself, "I feel that I am bound not to rob or murder, betray or steal, but why am I bound to promote the general happiness? If my own happiness lies in something else, why may I not give that the preference?"

Does Mill have an answer to this question, a question that would be asked by anyone who regarded his own individual happiness as his ultimate end? Answer it Mill must try to do, since he has employed the fact that all men do desire their individual happiness for its own sake and for nothing beyond itself, in order to establish happiness as the ultimate end that men do seek. He cannot dismiss this question lightly.

Coming from one of the world's most eminent logicians, the

answer Mill gives is a model of sophistry. It runs as follows: "No reason can be given why the general happiness is desirable [note: "desirable," not "desired"] except that each person, so far as he believes it to be attainable, desires his own happiness [note: "his own happiness" is what each person desires, not the "general happiness"]. This, however, being a fact, we have not only all the proof which the case admits of, but all which it is possible to require, that happiness is a good [granted]; that each person's happiness is a good to that person [granted, and more, it is his ultimate good]; and the general happiness, therefore [does "therefore" signify a valid logical sequitur?] a good to the aggregate of persons."

Not only is this plainly a non sequitur, as a matter of logic; it is also meaningless as a matter of fact, for even though an aggregate of persons may, as collectively organized, have a collective goal, it is not the object of their individual desires, nor can it be distributively identified with the diverse individual goals each seeks for himself.

In addition to suffering from the serious defect of its failure to distinguish between natural needs and conscious desires, and between real and apparent goods, utilitarianism is fatally hung up by positing two ultimate ends. The teleological and utilitarian ethics of common sense has only one basic normative principle, only one ultimate end, and only one primary moral obligation; and precisely because that one end, the *totum bonum* which is the same for all men, is a common good, and not the greatest good for the greatest number, common sense is able to pass from the obligations an individual has in the conduct of his own life, aiming at happiness, to the obligations he has in his conduct toward others, who are also aiming at the same happiness he seeks for himself.

The two ends that Mill fails properly to relate to one another can be properly related only when they are seen as, respectively, the ultimate end of the individual and the ultimate end of the state or political community. The ultimate end of the individual is only and always his own happiness (the *totum bonum commune hominis*). The ultimate end of the state or political community is the happiness of all its members—not the greatest good for the greatest number, but the general (or better, *common*) happiness that is the same for all men. Only the state can act for this end effectively and directly; the individual cannot. The individual is under the negative obligation not to interfere with or impair the pursuit of happiness by his fellow men; his only positive obligation toward them calls for conduct that indirectly promotes their pursuit of happiness by directly serving the good of the political community itself (the *bonum commune communitatis*), which is prerequisite to the state's functioning as a means to the "general happiness"— the ultimate good of all its individual members.

The happiness of the individual and the general happiness are both ends and both ultimate. This by itself creates no problem when their relationship is handled as Aristotle handled it. But Mill made an insoluble problem of it for himself by treating both ends as ultimate ends for one and the same agent—the individual.

The ethics of common sense, unlike either the deontological ethics of Kant or the utilitarianism of John Stuart Mill and some of his followers, is not an ethics that lays down rules of conduct by which a wide variety of particular acts can be judged good or bad, right or wrong; instead it is an ethics that judges particular acts mainly by reference to the moral quality of the habit or disposition that they manifest.

Given a man of good moral character, one who is disposed to seek everything that is really good for himself and to choose whatever means serve this end, any act he performs in accordance with his character tends to be a good act. Such a man can act badly only by acting out of character or against his character, and if by repetition of such acts, his habit or disposition itself is changed, he can become a man of bad moral character and thereby fail to achieve what is really good for himself.

Note 12. John Dewey's Mistake About Ultimate or Final Ends

When Dewey writes in *Reconstruction in Philosophy* that the end is not "a terminus or limit to be reached," and goes on to say that "growth itself is the only moral 'end,' " he fails to supplement his denial of terminal ends by developing a conception of an ultimate end that is purely normative. It must be added that, for Dewey, growth appears to function as that kind of end; and if Dewey had explicitly acknowledged it as an end that is not only normative but also ultimate (i.e., not a means to anything beyond itself), consistency would have led him to repudiate the reductionism of his naturalistic approach to normative questions and questions of value; for then he would have affirmed at least one good (growth) that was not good as a means, and so could not be converted into a matter of fact.

However, in *Human Nature and Conduct*, he completely rejects the very notion of an ultimate end or an end in itself, an end that is not a means. "There is no such thing," he writes, "as the single all-important end"; "ends," he says, "are, in fact, literally endless, forever coming into existence as new activities occasion new consequences. 'Endless ends' is a way of saying that there are no ends—that is, no fixed self-enclosed finalities."

POSTSCRIPT
Annotated Commentary on
Aristotle's *Nichomachean Ethics*

1

When I first thought of writing *The Time of Our Lives: The Ethics of Common Sense*, I conceived it as little more than a rewriting of the *Nicomachean Ethics* of Aristotle, expounding the moral insights I had learned over many years of reading and teaching it. The contribution I hoped to make I thought of mainly as a communication of its fundamental insights in language, imagery, and examples that have currency today, thus making them more accessible to the contemporary reader than they are in the pages of Aristotle.

In addition, I planned to convey only those portions of Aristotle's doctrine which have a universality that transcends time and place, and so have relevance for men living in any historic society and culture. I had one other criterion of selection. I would report only those Aristotelian formulations which seemed to me to be true and coherent.

After many readings of the *Ethics*, much remained that I could not assimilate to my purpose, because it was inconsistent with what I regarded as the controlling principles of Aristotle's doctrine, and much remained dark or obscure. Therefore, I would select only those points that I could expound clearly, defend as true, and put together into a consistent and coherent moral philosophy.

As this project developed in my mind and as the preparatory work for writing this book took the form of notes for lectures, I decided to keep my original intention a secret from the reader, mentioning it in a Postscript rather than in a Preface. I realized, of course, that for those readers who have studied Aristotle's *Ethics* and who have found it, as I have, a philosophical refinement of commonsense wisdom, it would be a poorly kept secret. But I also felt relatively sure that it would not be discovered by casual readers of the *Ethics*, or even by many contemporary philosophers whose interpretation and evaluation of that book differ remarkably from my own.

To preserve the secret, as much as it could be preserved, I refrained from making references to Aristotle's moral philosophy in the body of the book or in the notes to its chapters. The attentive reader will have observed, with some puzzlement perhaps, that—with one exception—all the citations of, or quotations from, Aristotle are on logical or metaethical points, not on matters germane to the substance of moral philosophy. . . .

The *Nicomachean Ethics* is a unique book in the Western tradition of moral philosophy. As Aristotle is uniquely the philosopher of common sense, so his moral philosophy is uniquely the ethics of common sense. It is the only ethics that is both teleological and deontological, the only ethics that is sound, practical, and undogmatic, offering what little normative wisdom there is for all men to be guided by, but refraining from laying down rules of conduct to cover the multifarious and contingent circumstances of human action.

In the history of Western moral thought, it is the only book centrally concerned and concerned throughout with the goodness of a whole human life, with the parts of this whole, and with putting the parts together in the right order and proportion. As far as I know, its only parallel is to be found outside of Western culture in the moral teachings of Confucius, which address themselves to the same problem and which offer a solution to it that also refines the wisdom of common sense—by means of aphorisms rather than, as in Aristotle's case, by means of analysis and argument.[1]* . . .

My book . . . contains formulations, analytical distinctions, arguments, and elaborations that cannot be found in the *Ethics*; in addition, the conceptions and insights taken from Aristotle are not simply adopted without modification, but adapted to fit together into a theoretical framework that is somewhat different from Aristotle's. If it appears immodest for me to claim more originality for what is set forth in these pages, it would be dishonest for me to pretend that I am merely translating into twentieth-century idiom the wisdom I have found in a book written almost 2,500 years ago.

The most accurate description of what I have done, it seems to me, would be to say that certain things to be found in Aristotle's *Ethics* constitute my point of departure and control the general direction of my thought, but that I have gone further along the line of thinking about moral problems laid down by Aristotle—adding innovations to his theory, as well as extending and modifying it. Much of what is new or altered in my formulation of the ethics of common sense results from my effort to defend its wisdom against philosophical objections that were unknown to Aristotle, or to correct the misconceptions, misunderstandings, and ignorances that have dominated the scene in the last few hundreds years.

However, even in dealing with the multifarious errors in modern and contemporary moral philsophy, I have been able to employ critical tools I have found in Aristotle. As an indirect confirmation of this, let me call attention to the fact that in criticizing such leading modern and contemporary moral philosophers as Immanuel Kant, J.S. Mill . . . and John Dewey, I have, usually without mentioning Aristotle's name or citing his work, pointed out misunderstandings of conceptions fundamental to Aristotelian doctrine or ignorance of distinctions and neglect of insights that, had they been learned from Aristotle, would have prevented these modern authors from making the mistakes they have made. They all certainly read the *Nicomachean Ethics* as students and most

*See the Endnotes at the end of this Appendix.

of them reconsidered it in the years of their own mature development; but the evidence is plain that for one reason or another, they read it very poorly, or perhaps I should say that their reading of Aristotle and their interpretation of his thought are as different from mine as if they and I were reading utterly different books.

I know of few books that have been as variously interpreted as the *Nicomachean Ethics*. Many of the interpretations—in fact, most of them—make it out to be worth studying as a monument in the history of thought, or worth criticizing in order to point out errors we should avoid, but hardly a book that contains the one right approach to moral problems and more wisdom and truth in the solution of them than any book written since the fourth century B.C.

Among contemporary commentaries on Aristotle's *Ethics*, even the few interpretations that commend his approach or praise certain of his insights do not go all out in defense of his doctrine. I know of only one book—Henry Veatch's *Rational Man*—that not only adopts Aristotle's approach without reservation, but also expounds and defends the wisdom and truth to be found in his doctrine, while at the same time acknowledging that Aristotle, like every other great philosopher, made mistakes that should not be perpetuated out of reverence for his authority.

Scholars often argue for the correctness of their interpretation of a text; scholarly literature is full of controversy over the correct reading of this set of passages or that. Adjudicating such arguments or taking part in such controversies is not the business of a philosopher. Faced with the many divergent interpretations of the *Nicomachean Ethics*, I have no right or wish to claim that my reading of it has so perfectly grasped the meaning of every passage in that complicated text that I know with assurance precisely what Aristotle thought. . . . The meaning I attach to the words on this page or that may diverge from or even distort what Aristotle had in mind. I have already confessed that there is much in the book that remains dark or obscure to me, and that I have found many passages the apparent meaning of which I cannot easily reconcile with my interpretation of other passages that I have construed as expressing the controlling insights of the book.

What, then, can I claim for my reading of Aristotle's *Ethics*?

Only this: (1) that it is an interpretation which sets forth a moral philosophy that is sound, practical, and undogmatic; (2) that it is an interpretation which, applying philosophical, not scholarly, criteria for judging what is morally true and wise, separates the wheat from the chaff and rejects what cannot be assimilated to a coherent ethical theory that is both teleological and deontological and that is based on the specific nature of man; and (3) that the ethical doctrine which emerges from this interpretation deserves to be called Aristotelian even if it does not represent the doctrine of Aristotle's *Ethics* in its entirety; or, in other words, that the moral wisdom and truths I have expounded as the ethics of common sense can be attributed to Aristotle more than to any other philosopher [2] . . . .

Some readers of these works, especially Aristotle's medieval commentators and their modern counterparts, have found the whole a seamless fabric of clear and coherent doctrine. I am unpersuaded by their efforts to make it appear so. Some readers, in modern times and especially in our own day, have gone to the opposite extreme—finding nothing but unresolvable difficulties or perplexities, irreconcilable strains of thought and inadequately expounded views. I cannot accept the picture they present, nor the estimate it implies.

I myself have, from time to time, adopted a third alternative, which is probably as untenable. It is the old myth, for which there is certainly no clear or sufficient evidence, that these works originated in lectures that Aristotle gave to his students; that in the course of these lectures Aristotle was engaged in a systematic effort to explore for the first time the ethical and political dimensions of moral philosophy; that in the process of doing so, his own thought gradually developed and changed, with important insights and discoveries occurring at a later stage in the process, discoveries which called for the modification or even rejection of tentative formulations expressed at an earlier stage; that when he had finished giving his lectures, he had not yet reached the point where he was in possession of a clear-cut and coherent doctrine that he could expound systematically; that his lectures were either handed down to his students in manuscript, or taken down in extensive notes by them, compiled as treatises, and edited, but *not by Ar-*

istotle himself; and that if Aristotle had reread these compilations and then himself had written the books based on his lectures about ethics and politics, he would have produced two books in moral philosophy quite different from the ones we now have.

The difficulty with this myth, quite apart from any question about its factual authenticity, is that it might lead the person who adopted it to claim that he knew how Aristotle would have written the *Ethics* and the *Politics*, if he had carefully studied the notes based on his lectures and revised what he found there in order to present a clear and coherent doctrine, set forth demonstratively rather than dialectically and in the logical order of exposition rather than in the order of discovery.

This would be tantamount to claiming that one had the inside track to all of Aristotle's thought, which is as impossible to support as the claim that one has the only correct interpretation of his works. What claim, then, can I make for the passages from the *Ethics* and *Politics* that I am going to quote in support of the proposition that the ethics of common sense expounded in this book is Aristotelian in tenor, even if it does not represent the whole of Aristotle's thought and may even run counter to certain aspects of it?

A letter William James wrote in 1900 to a graduate student at Harvard who had written a doctoral dissertation on his philosophy will help me to explain what I propose to do. "As a Ph.D. thesis," James told Miss S., "your essay is supreme, but why don't you go farther? You take utterances of mine written at different dates, for different audiences belonging to different universes of discourse, and string them together as the abstract elements of a total philosophy which you then show to be inwardly incoherent. This is splendid philology . . . [but] your use of the method only strengthens the impression I have got from reading criticisms of my 'pragmatic' account of 'truth,' that the whole Ph.D. industry of building an author's meaning out of separate texts leads nowhere, *unless you have first grasped his center of vision, by an act of imagination* . . . Not by proving their inward incoherence does one refute philosophies—every human being is incoherent—but only by superseding them by other philosophies more satisfactory. Your wonderful technical skill ought to serve you in good stead if you would exchange the philological kind of criticism for constructive work. I fear however that you won't—the iron may have bitten too deeply into your soul!!" The letter is signed: "Yours with mingled admiration and abhorrence, Wm. James." [3]

If Aristotle were alive today to read the commentaries that have been written about his philosophy, I could imagine him feeling about most of them what James felt about the efforts of Miss S. Therefore, I am going to try [here] to follow James's excellent advice—by selecting those passages in Aristotle's *Ethics* and *Politics* that I regard as controlling any effort to get at the center of his vision.

If, in the view of others, this is too much to claim, I am prepared to fall back on more modest claims and ones I think can be defended: first, that the passages I am going to cite must be given a controlling position in any interpretation of Aristotle's thought; and, second, that the insights expressed in these passages do in fact control the development of the moral philosophy I have expounded in this book, and justify my calling the ethics of common sense Aristotelian, even if it is not identical in content with Aristotle's *Ethics*.

I will proceed in the next five sections . . . to quote and interpret what I have called the "controlling passages," and to indicate how other, apparently conflicting passages can, by interpretation, be reconciled with them. Then, in a final section, I will conclude with a few brief observations concerning the fate of Aristotle's *Ethics* in the history of moral philosophy in the West.

2

I have said that Aristotle's *Ethics* is both teleological and deontological. An ethical theory is teleological if it posits a single ultimate end as its first principle, and it is deontological if it makes the good which is this ultimate end the primary object of a categorical moral obligation that is universally binding on all men in the same way.

For Aristotle, the single ultimate end is happiness conceived as the goodness of a human life as a whole. So conceived, happiness is the *totum bonum* (the whole of goods), not the *summum bonum* (the highest among the various partial goods that are components of happiness or parts of the whole). As the *totum bonum*, happiness or a whole good life is a normative, not a terminal, end—an end that takes a complete life to achieve, and therefore an end that is not achieved at any moment in the time of our lives.

Therefore, happiness is neither experienceable nor enjoyable, for the satisfactions of desire that we experience and enjoy occur in passing moments of time. In contrast to happiness, all other goods—all of them less than the whole good and all of them parts of happiness—can be possessed and enjoyed during the course of our lives.

The passages in the *Nicomachean Ethics (NE)* that I am now about to cite reveal what, in my judgment, is the most distinctive feature of that book and what makes it unique among treatises in moral philosophy. It is the only ethical theory in which a good life as a temporal whole is the controlling or normative end of all action, and in which the goodness of particular types of activity or the goodness of the results they achieve is measured by their contribution to making a whole life good, each of these partial goods being a means to that end and all of them together being that end in the process of becoming.

I will postpone until Section 3 the citation of the texts that give us Aristotle's enumeration of the partial goods or means to happiness and that indicate which among them is the highest good, and then, in Section 4, I will cite textual evidence to show that, in Aristotle's view, we are under a categorical moral obligation to make a really good life by choosing rightly—or virtuously—the activities or the results of action by which we can make our lives good as a whole.

"If we do not choose everything for the sake of something else (for at that rate the process would go on to infinity and our desires would be empty and vain), then there is some end of the things we do which we desire for its own sake—everything else being desired for the sake of this. Clearly, this must be the good and the chief good."[1] Some goods may be merely means, some goods may be ends as well as means, but of the goods that are ends, only one is an end that is never a means, and it is, therefore, the ultimate or final end. "We call that which is in itself worthy of pursuit more final than that which is worthy of pursuit for the sake of something else; and that which is never desirable for the sake of something else is more final than the things that are desirable both in themselves and for the sake of something else. Therefore, we call final without qualification [i.e., the ultimate end, absolutely speaking] that which is desirable in itself and never for the sake of something else."[2]

This, Aristotle declares, is happiness—the good "we always seek for its own sake and never for the sake of something else," whereas every other good, even those we desire for their own sakes, "we seek also for the sake of happiness, judging that by means of them we shall become happy."[3] Aristotle then points out that when we speak of happiness as the ultimate end, we must be careful not to speak of it as *a* good, but rather as *the* good. Although he himself has called it "the chief good," he makes clear that it is not to be thought of as the highest good, but as the whole of goods. Happiness is the chief good only in the sense that "it is the most desirable of all things without being counted as one good among others." His argument to support this point is unanswerable. If happiness were counted as one good among others, even though it were the highest or best of all such goods, "it would become more desirable by the addition of even the least of goods," in which case happiness by itself would not be the most desirable good, for the combination of happiness (as just one good) with any other additional good would be more desirable than happiness by itself, since "among goods the greater is always more desirable." Therefore, happiness as the ultimate end is not *a* good, but *the* good—that whole of goods to which nothing can be added and from which "nothing is lacking."[4]

---

[1] Aristotle, *Nicomachean Ethics*, I, 2, 1094ª18–22.
[2] *NE*, I, 7, 1097ª30–35.
[3] Ibid., 1097ª37–1097ᵇ6.
[4] Ibid., 1097ᵇ15–22.

The foregoing argument is repeated in Book X, where Aristotle says that "it is by an argument of this kind that Plato proves the good *not* to be pleasure; he argues that the life of pleasure is more desirable with wisdom than without it, and that if the combination of the two is better, then pleasure is not *the* good, for *the* good cannot become more desirable by the addition of anything to it."[5] Aristotle then adds that no other partial good, any more than pleasure, can be *the* good if it is just one good among others, to which other goods can be added. Thus, as we shall see presently, the intellectual activity which, in Book X, Aristotle regards as the highest good (the *summum bonum*) does not constitute happiness (the *totum bonum*), for it, like pleasure, is only one good among others, and can be made more desirable by the addition of such other goods as wealth, health, and pleasure.

Happiness, Aristotle says again and again, is a good life as a whole; it consists in living well by choosing rightly among the various activities that can occupy our time and that can achieve certain results, each of which is only one good among others. However one describes the constituents of happiness, Aristotle insists that to any enumeration of its component parts, we must always "add 'in a complete life'; for one swallow does not make a summer, nor does one day; and so one day, or a short time, does not make a man happy."[6]

That is why children and youths cannot be called happy. If we ever attribute happiness to them in view of their promise or the good fortune that smiles on the beginning of their lives, it is "by reason of the hopes we have for them" not because they have achieved happiness, for that "requires a complete life, since many changes occur in life, and all manner of chances, and the most prosperous may fall into great misfortunes in old age."[7]

Aristotle confirms this in his discussion of Solon's observation that one can accurately judge the goodness of a human life only when it has been completed, but not while it is still in process.[8]

[5] *NE*, X, 2, 1172ª28–32.
[6] *NE*, I, 7, 1098ª17–18; cf. X, 7, 1177ᵇ23–24.
[7] *NE*, I, 9, 1100ª1–7.
[8] See *NE*, I, 10, 1100ª10–1100ᵇ10.

Of a living man, we can never say *without qualification* that he is happy; only when a man's life is over can we say that it was a happy or a good life. While the individual is still engaged in trying to make a good life for himself, we can say only that the signs suggest that he is succeeding, that he is becoming happy, or that his life is becoming a good one. Happiness consists in living and acting well, under fortunate circumstances, "not for some chance period but throughout a complete life." At any moment in our lives, "the future remains obscure to us"; one's fortunes and one's character may change for better or for worse. As we shall see, good fortune and good character are essential conditions of happiness. So when we call a living man happy, our doing so is not only descriptive of his past but also predictive of his future: we are saying that he is one "in whom these conditions are *and are to be* fulfilled."[9]

3

Aristotle names a relatively small number of goods, each of which is a component of happiness—an element in the *totum bonum* that is a good life as a whole. A good life, he says, is impossible without a decent minimum of external goods, which include not only the means of subsistence but other forms of prosperity, some of which are conferred by good fortune.[10]

It is impossible without the goods of the body—health and vigor.[11] It is impossible without pleasure, not only the pleasures of sense, but the pleasures inherent in certain types of activity.[12] It is impossible without friends or loved ones.[13] It is impossible without what Aristotle calls "the goods of soul"—the goods I have called the goods of self-improvement. These, as a class, stand

[9] Ibid., 1101ª15–21; italics added.
[10] See *NE*, I, 8, 1099ª31–1099ᵇ8; I, 10, 1101ª16; VII, 13, 1153ᵇ18–24; X, 8, 1179ª2–12.
[11] See *NE*, VII, 13, 1153ᵇ17; X, 8, 1178ᵇ34–35.
[12] See *NE*, VII, 13, 1153ᵇ13–15; VII, 14, 1154ª1–22.
[13] See *NE*, IX, 8, 1169ᵇ3–22; IX, 11, 1171ª34–1171ᵇ27.

highest among the partial goods that constitute the *totum bonum*.[14]

All the mistakes men make about happiness or the good life consist either in identifying it with one or another of the partial goods or in not correctly ordering these partial goods in relation to one another.[15] The fact that each of these partial goods is something happiness depends on may explain but does not lessen the mistake of regarding any of them as the one thing in which happiness consists. The fact that each of these goods corresponds to a natural human need does not make them all coordinate or of equal value, for some of them, as Aristotle points out, serve as means to other ends as well as being means to happiness itself, and some, such as the goods of self-perfection, are not only means to happiness but good in themselves, as ends to be sought for their own sake.

In addition to naming the goods that are indispensable to happiness or a good life, Aristotle also names, with one exception, the basic types of activity by which these goods are obtained: wealth, by *work*; pleasure, by *play* or amusement; friendships and the goods of self-improvement, by *leisure*. The one exception is Aristotle's failure to name the various activities by which the bodily goods of health and vigor are obtained, for which I have employed the omnibus term *sleep*. Some of these activities, including the therapeutic form of play which Aristotle calls "relaxation," are mentioned in Book X of the *Ethics*[16] and are discussed again in the *Politics*.[17]

Aristotle's ordering of these activities confirms his ordering of the goods with which they are associated. What he says about therapeutic play applies to all the activities I have grouped together under sleep; giving us health and bodily vigor, they are for the sake of work—either subsistence-work or leisure-work. Subsistence-work, in turn, is for the sake of leisure-work, and while a

---

[14] See *NE*, I, 8, 1098ᵇ14–16.

[15] See *NE*, I, 4; I, 5; I, 8; VII, 13, 1153ᵇ20–24; VII, 14, 1154ᵃ8–21; X, 3, 1174ᵃ1–14; X, 6, 1176ᵇ8–1177ᵃ12.

[16] See ibid., Chapters 6 and 7.

[17] See Aristotle, *Politics*, Book VII, Chapters 14–15; Book VIII, Chapters 3, 5.

certain amount of play simply for the pleasure inherent in it is a necessary element in a good life, it should be engaged in with moderation in order to allow as much free time as possible for the self-cultivating pursuits of leisure.

Under the guidance of the controlling insight that happiness is *the* good *(totum bonum)*, not the *highest* good *(summum bonum)*, in which case it would be only one good among others, we can see that happiness does not consist in self-perfection, or the goods of self-improvement, even though these constitute the highest among partial goods. The same insight applies to leisure among the activities that occupy our time, and to that special form of leisure—speculative activity, contemplation, or thinking and knowing for the sake of thinking and knowing—which Aristotle prizes for its contribution to happiness.

Aristotle's views concerning the principal forms of leisure were somewhat conditioned and colored by the cultural circumstances of an aristocratic, agrarian, slave-holding society, but that need not prevent us from divesting his conception of the good life of its local trappings and universalizing its terms so that they apply not just to an elite living under certain historic conditions but to all men everywhere at all times.

He says, for example, that men who have sufficient property and slaves to attend to chores, so that they do not have to work for a living or operate their estates, should "occupy themselves with philosophy or with politics."[18] This need not be read narrowly to signify the activity of the philosopher or the activity of the statesmen as Aristotle thought of these pursuits—activities which, in other places, he contrasts as the speculative or contemplative life, on the one hand, and as the political or active life, on the other.[19]

The word "philosophy" can be broadly interpreted to stand for all the arts and sciences—for the whole range of creative intellectual work by which the individual himself learns and also, perhaps, makes some contribution to culture as a result of his learning.

[18] *Politics*, I, 8, 1255b37–38.
[19] See *NE*, I, 5, 1095b18; X, 7, 1177b15–1178a2; X, 8, 1178a8–13; and cf. *Politics*, VII, 2, 1324a27–32; VII, 3, 1325b15–23.

The word "politics" can be similarly extended to cover all the institutions of society and all public or quasi-public affairs, including those of business and other corporate enterprises, involving the individual in action as well as in thought, yet constituting genuine leisure for the individual only to the extent that his intellectual involvement results in learning or some other aspect of personal growth.

Thus, broadly interpreted, philosophy and politics would appear to be the two principal forms of leisure, even though they may not exhaust every variety of leisure pursuit, among which must be included the activities concerned with love and friendship.

The man who is neither a philosopher nor a statesman in Aristotle's sense of these terms is not precluded from engagement in the pursuits of leisure. Considering the diversity of human aptitudes or talents and the wide range of individual abilities, it still remains the case that, for every man, leisure, in one form or another, is supreme among human activities, and the resulting goods of self-improvement constitute the most important ingredient in a good life.

Aristotle's handling of the question whether speculative or political activity makes the greater contribution to happiness leaves the matter unresolved; there are passages, among those cited above, in which he favors the one, and passages in which he favors the other. However, a resolution is obtainable by altering the question somewhat. Considering an individual's talents and temperament, as well as the external circumstances of his life, what form of leisure-work will contribute most to his learning—to the growth of his mind and to the development of his personality? That, *for him*, is the highest form of leisure; *for someone else*, it may be something else; *for each man*, happiness is to be achieved to the highest possible degree by the fullest engagement in what is for him the highest form of leisure-work.

----- 4 -----

It is in one way easy to understand why modern philosophers, beginning with Kant, have regarded Aristotle's eudaemonistic eth-

ics or ethics of happiness as the very opposite of a deontological
ethics, or an ethics of categorical obligation. There can be no
question that it gives primacy to the good rather than to the right.
It proceeds mainly in terms of the desirable rather than in terms
of the dutiful. It appears to lay down no moral laws: the pages
of the *Nicomachean Ethics* are almost totally devoid of explicitly
formulated rules of conduct, and of criteria for judging whether
a particular action is right or wrong.

Nevertheless, as I will now try to show, to dismiss Aristotle's
doctrine, as Kant and others following him have done, as purely
pragmatic or utilitarian, in the sense that it appeals only to what
men do in fact consciously desire without considering what they
ought to desire, represents a profound misreading of the book.

This misreading is remarkable because it fails to observe points
that furnish the reader with controlling insights for interpreting
the book as a whole. First of all, there is the fact so pervasive that
it is very difficult to miss, namely, that Aristotle, in dealing with
the diverse opinions men hold concerning happiness, directs his
efforts toward discovering and formulating the one right conception of happiness. He is clearly denying that any version of the
good life is as sound as any other, and just as clearly affirming
that happiness, rightly conceived, is the same for all men precisely
because, regardless of their individual differences, they are all
human beings, the same in their specific nature. He rejects the
opinion that happiness consists solely in a life of pleasure, a life
of money-making, a life filled with external goods, a life devoted
to the attainment of public honor or prestige or power over other
men, and even a life that consists exclusively in being virtuous or
in the pursuits of leisure.[20] The reason in each case is the same.
With the exception of arbitrary power over other men, each of
the things mentioned is *a* good or is associated with the attainment
of a good, but it is not *the* good, and therefore it is only a part
of happiness, not the whole of it. Correctly conceived as the *totum*

---

[20] See *NE*, I, 4, 1095^{a}15–27; I, 5; I, 8, 1098^{b}20–29, 1099^{a}32–1099^{b}8; VII,
13, 1153^{b}13–24; X, 3, 1174^{a}1–12; X, 6, 1176^{b}27–1177^{a}11; X, 8, 1178^{b}32–
1179^{a}12; and cf. *Politics*, I, 9, 1257^{b}35–1258^{a}7; VII, 1, 1324^{a}1–2; VII, 3,
1325^{a}20–33; VII, 13, 1332^{a}17–27.

bonum, happiness consists in all the things that are really good for a man; none, not even the least of these, can be omitted if the individual is to achieve a good life, but they are not all of equal value, and so he must seek to relate and mix the ingredients of happiness in the right order and proportion.

An ethics of happiness which insists upon seeking the one right end (happiness correctly conceived as the *totum bonum*) and seeking it in the right way (by correctly relating and proportioning the partial goods that enter into it) is clearly a moral philosophy that declares what a man *ought* to seek and how he *ought* to seek it.

This controlling insight is confirmed in a number of ways. It is confirmed by a statement in the *Politics*, in which Aristotle says that the successful pursuit of happiness depends upon two things: "one of them is the choice of the right end and aim of action, and the other the discovery of the actions which are means to it; for the means and the end may agree or disagree."[21] It is also confirmed by all the passages in the *Nicomachean Ethics*, in which Aristotle, considering the role of pleasure in the good life, distinguishes between good and bad pleasures, and between a right and wrong pursuit of them.[22] Commenting on the pleasures of sense, he points out that one can have too much of these goods. "The bad man is bad by reason of pursuing the excess, not by reason of pursuing the needed pleasures (for *all* men enjoy in some way or other both dainty foods and wines and sexual intercourse, *but not all men do so as they ought*)."[23] Most of all, it is confirmed by Aristotle's use of the distinction between the real and the apparent good.

With regard to the desire for the good, Aristotle points out that "some think that it is for the real good; others, for the apparent good. Now those who say that the real good is the object of desire must admit in consequence that that which the man who does not choose aright seeks is not an object of desire . . . while those who

[21] *Politics*, VII, 13, 1331ᵇ27–31.
[22] See, for example, *NE*, II, 3, 1104ᵇ8–12, 30–35; X, 5, 1175ᵇ22–35, 1176ᵃ15–29.
[23] *NE*, VII, 14, 1154ᵃ16–18; italics added.

say that the apparent good is the object of desire must claim that there is nothing which is naturally an object of desire, but only that which appears good to each man—and different things appear good to different individuals."[24]

Aristotle then goes on to suggest that the apparent good is that which men in fact consciously desire, whether they ought to or not, and the real good is that which they in fact naturally desire and ought consciously to desire. Hence the difficulty is resolved; both the real and the apparent good are objects of desire, but whereas the former is both the object of natural desire and that which men ought consciously to desire, the latter is only the object of conscious desire. "That which is really good is an object of desire for the good man [that is, the man who desires as he ought to desire], while any chance thing may be an object of desire [an apparent good] for the bad man."[25]

If real goods—the objects of natural desire—ought to be desired, and nothing but real goods ought to be desired, then the right conception of happiness—the good life that all men ought to seek and that is the same for all men because they are men—must be a conception of it as constituted by the sum of real goods. Aristotle's remark that "the end appears to each man in a form corresponding to his moral character"[26] clearly means that only the morally virtuous man—the man of right desire, the man who chooses aright—will be motivated by the right conception of happiness as the end to be pursued. The morally virtuous man is one whose will is aimed at the end that every man ought to seek, and whose actions in pursuit of that end are chosen as they ought to be chosen in relation and proportion to one another.

If any further confirmation were required to show that the *Nicomachean Ethics* is at once deontological and teleological—that it prescribes categorical oughts with respect to the ultimate end and the necessary means thereto—the prima facie evidence

[24] *NE*, III, 4, 1113ª15–23.
[25] Ibid., III, 4, 1113ª25–27.
[26] Ibid., III, 5, 1114ª32–1114ᵇ1.

for it lies in the indispensability of virtue to happiness, the good life, or living well.

It is so clear in Aristotle's mind that happiness can be rightly conceived and rightly pursued only by a person who has the habit of desiring and choosing aright (such good disposition of will, or habit of right desire and choice, being moral virtue), that he allows an elliptical definition of happiness as "activity in accordance with virtue" or as "virtuous activity"[27] to serve in place of the more exact and complete statement that happiness or the good life consists in possessing all the real goods that are the objects the morally virtuous man desires, as he ought, in the right order and proportion; for the morally virtuous man is one who aims at the end that he ought to seek and chooses the means to it in the way they ought to be chosen.[28]

Still another way of expanding the elliptical statement that happiness is activity in accordance with virtue or is virtuous activity is to say that the activities of a good life all aim at real goods, or at apparent goods only when they are innocuous, and these activities contribute to making a whole life really good because they and the goods they aim at have been sought and chosen virtuously, that is, in the right order and proportion.

Moral virtue is not itself a component part of happiness, except insofar as it is one aspect of self-perfection or self-improvement. Its special relation to happiness consists in its being not the highest good, but rather the chief instrumental or operative means to achieving a good life. All the goods that are needed for a good life are either the goods of chance or the goods of choice. For some of the constituent elements of happiness, we depend wholly on the chance favors of fortune, including the good fortune of living in a just and benevolent society, but for those elements essential to a good life that depend wholly or even partly on our own free choices, moral virtue is the decisive factor.[29]

[27] NE, I, 7, 1098a27; I, 9, 1099b26.
[28] See especially NE, I, 10; I, 13, 1102a5–6; X, 6, 1176b37; and cf. Politics, VII, 2, 1324a1–2; VII, 13, 1332a8–25.
[29] See Politics, VII, 2, 1323b25–29; and cf. NE, I, 10, 1100b23–32.

—— 5 ——

Since moral virtue plays so critical a role in Aristotle's theory of the good life, as the *sine qua non* of a man's effective pursuit of happiness, it is necessary to clarify two points that can be and usually are overlooked in the reading of the *Nicomachean Ethics*.

The first concerns Aristotle's use of the phrase "virtuous activity." It might be thought that virtuous activity is a special type of activity, as work, play, and leisure are distinct types of activity. But that is not the case. At the end of Book I, Aristotle, projecting an extended discussion of virtue that will occupy Books II–VI, points out that "some of the virtues are intellectual and others moral."[30] Although the intellectual virtues can be inculcated by teaching as moral virtue cannot be, both consist in habits—in stable dispositions of mind or character.[31]

In the case of the intellectual virtues—take, for example, science or art—the virtue is a habit or disposition of the mind to act in a certain way. The scientist or the artist is a man whose mind can perform well certain operations that the man who is not a scientist or an artist either cannot perform at all or certainly cannot perform well. Excellence in a certain type of intellectual activity will be found in those men who possess the appropriate intellectual virtues—the good habits or dispositions of mind that give rise to such activities.

Moral virtue, in contrast, is a habit of willing and choosing, not a habit of acting in a certain specific way. It is, Aristotle writes, "a state of character concerned with choice."[32] Specific activities of all sorts, intellectual and otherwise, are the things men choose to engage in or avoid in order to achieve the end that they seek. The habit of seeking a certain end and the habit of choosing and ordering activities in a certain way to gain that end is the habit of willing and choosing which is moral virtue.

[30] *NE*, I, 13, 1103ª5.
[31] See *NE*, II, 1, 1103ª15–25.
[32] *NE*, II, 6, 1106ᵇ37.

In one sense, of course, willing and choosing are actions, but they are not activities in the same sense in which working, playing, and leisuring are activities, nor in the sense in which scientific or artistic operations are specific forms of leisure activity. Thus, when the reference is to moral, not intellectual, virtue, the phrase "virtuous activity" must be treated as an elliptical expression that is short for "virtuously chosen activities," and this, like the phrase "activity in accordance with virtue," needs further expansion as follows: "activities directed to the right end and chosen in the right order and proportion."

The morally virtuous man is one who has a good character. This consists in a habit or disposition with respect to the end that he seeks and the means that he chooses; and the *goodness* of this habit of willing and choosing, which makes it a *virtue* rather than a vice, consists in its being a disposition to will the right end or the end that he ought to seek and to choose the means in the right way or in the way that he ought to choose them in order to achieve the end. Living as he ought by habit, the man of good character has no need of rules of conduct; moral virtue as good habit dispenses with rules.

This brings us to the second and more important point that requires clarification. Since an intellectual virtue is the habit of a certain specific type of intellectual activity, there can be a number of distinct intellectual virtues. But since moral virtue is a disposition to will the right end and to choose the means for achieving it in the right way, there cannot be a number of existentially distinct moral virtues, but only a plurality of analytically distinct aspects of one and the same existential state of good moral character.

The controlling text on this point is to be found in the last chapter of Book VI, though even there Aristotle himself uses the word "virtue" in the plural rather than the singular, and the passage is further complicated by an ambiguity in Aristotle's use of *phronesis* for two quite distinct qualities of mind: (a) moral wisdom, which consists in a correct understanding of the *ultimate end* to be sought and of the *means in general* for achieving it; and (b) prudence, which consists in the habit of reaching a sound judgment in *this particular case* about which is the better or best of alternative means for achieving the end. English translators usually render *phronesis* by "practical wisdom"; but wisdom *(sophia)*—whether speculative or practical—in Aristotle's understanding of it is always restricted to universal principles.

In the practical or moral order, the principles with which wisdom is concerned are constituted by the *ultimate end* and the *means in general* (the means to happiness universally conceived). Deliberation about which is the better or the best of available means *in a particular case* does not come within the scope of moral or practical wisdom. It belongs to another habit of mind— the habit of prudence, which is a habit of proceeding in the right way to reach a decision about the means in a particular case, that is, by taking counsel, by weighing the alternatives, by deliberating carefully, and so on.[33]

The only justification for calling prudence "practical wisdom" lies in the word "practical," not in the word "wisdom," for the word "practical" does refer to action; action always takes place in particular cases; and it is the particular case with which prudence is always concerned, as wisdom never is.

With these clarifications in analysis and vocabulary, let me now render the passage I regard as giving us the controlling insight for understanding Aristotle's theory of moral virtue, in itself, as a single habit of will and choice, and in its relation to moral wisdom, on the one hand, and to prudence on the other.

Book VI ends with the statement: "It is clear, then, from what has been said that it is not possible to be good [morally virtuous] in the strict sense without being morally wise, nor prudent without being good [having moral virtue]. In this way we may refute the dialectical argument whereby it might be contended that the virtues [moral virtues] exist in separation from each other. . . . This is possible in the case of certain temperamental qualities [such as fearlessness, on the one hand, and mildness on the other], but not in the case of that attribute with respect to which a man is called without qualification morally good."[34]

Aristotle's rejection of the view that the moral virtues can exist

---

[33] See *NE*, VI, 7, 1141^{b}8–23; VI, 8, 1142^{a}20–31; VI, 9, 1142^{b}3–35.
[34] *NE*, VI, 13, 1144^{b}30–1145^{a}2.

in separation from each other makes it impossible to hold that there can be two existentially separate moral virtues, such as fortitude or courage, on the one hand, and temperance on the other, as there can be two existentially separate temperamental qualities, such as fearlessness and mildness.

The plurality of names used in the case of moral virtue (and there is a large number of them in Books III and IV, of which fortitude and temperance are the principal ones) must, therefore, be interpreted to signify a plurality of analytically distinct aspects of one and the same good habit or state of good moral character, not a plurality of existentially distinct moral habits, any one of which can be possessed in the absence of others.

The reason for the existential unity of moral virtue should be clear from what has been said earlier about a good moral character. It consists, as we have seen, in a habit of right desire, which is to say a habit of desiring as one ought, a disposition to will the right end and to choose the right means in the right order and proportion.

Since there is only one right end to be sought and only one right order and proportion of the means for achieving the end, there is only one habit of right desire and that one habit is moral virtue, complete and entire. We can read this insight back into the passage in Book I, where Aristotle, having said that the good life consists of activity in accordance with virtue, then adds: "and *if* there is more than one virtue, then in accordance with *complete* virtue."[35]

From what has been said, it should also be clear why it is impossible for a man to be morally good without being morally wise, since one could not have the habit of right desire without having an understanding of the right end to be sought and knowledge of the means in general for achieving it, together with an understanding of how those means should be ordered and proportioned. Such knowledge and understanding of the end and the means constitute moral wisdom.

But moral wisdom can be possessed in two ways—*explicitly*,

[35] *NE*, I, 7, 1098ª28; cf. I, 10, 1101ª15; italics added.

in the propositional form typical of intellectual cognition, or *implicitly*, without propositional or argumentative expression. The man of moral virtue or good moral character must certainly possess moral wisdom implicitly, but whether he must also possess it explicitly, in the propositional and argumentative form appropriate to intellectual cognition, is doubtful. This is not to deny that he would be better off if he did.

The reverse point that Aristotle makes at the end of Book VI is on one interpretation true and on another interpretation false. In the passage already cited, the usual translation has it that it is impossible to be "practically wise without moral virtue," as well as "morally good without practical wisdom." We have just seen that it is impossible to be morally good (have the habit of right desire) without having moral wisdom implicitly, though it remains questionable whether one must also have it explicitly. But the reverse relationship between moral virtue and "practical wisdom" holds only when "practical wisdom" is understood as referring to *prudence*, not when it is understood as referring to *moral wisdom*.

It is impossible to be prudent without being morally good; prudence as distinguished from mere cleverness or shrewdness consists in the habit of proceeding in the right way to reach a decision about the means in a particular case *only* if the choice is among means all directed to the right end. A thief or a murderer may exhibit that counterfeit of prudence which Aristotle calls cleverness or shrewdness, but it is not true prudence because the means with which it is concerned in the particular case are not means to the right end.[36]

But while it is impossible to be prudent without being morally good, it is certainly possible to be morally wise—in a purely intellectual way—without being a man of good moral character or of moral virtue. Being able to recite the truths of moral philosophy or even being intellectually convinced of them does not necessarily carry with it that stable disposition of the will—that habit of right desire—which constitutes moral virtue or a man's good moral

---

[36] See *NE*, VI, 12, 1144^{a}25–29; VI, 13, 1144^{b}1–16, 1145^{a}5–7.

character. If only that were the case, then imparting moral wisdom to the young by the teaching of a sound moral philosophy would produce morally virtuous men, but we know moral virtue is not acquired in this way. Rather it is by discipline and training, by practice and habituation, that morally virtuous individuals are formed.[37] Aristotle is careful not to give specific rules for the cultivation of moral virtue, just as he is careful not to rely on teaching moral philosophy to the young.[38]

Among the many aspects of moral virtue discussed in Books II–IV, fortitude and temperance are the principal ones. Virtue, Aristotle says, is "concerned with pleasures and pains," for "it is on account of pleasures that we do the wrong things, and on account of pains that we abstain from doing the right ones."[39] It is in these terms that he differentiates between temperance and fortitude as distinct aspects of moral virtue. Temperance consists in a disposition to give up immediate pleasures that are only apparent goods in order to achieve real goods that are often remote; fortitude consists in a disposition to suffer the pains or withstand the difficulties that are often attendant upon doing the things one ought to do for the sake of making one's whole life really good. Both are aspects of one and the same basic habit of choice—the disposition to prefer a good life in the long run (however hard it may be to work for that end) to a good and an easy time here and now (however pleasant that may be from moment to moment).

There is only one other principal aspect of moral virtue, and that is justice, which is treated in Book V. Here Aristotle distinguishes between justice in general, which is nothing but moral virtue as directed toward the good of other men, and the special forms of justice that are the qualities of human transactions, such as exchanges and distributions, or human laws and other acts of government. The latter, which is one place he refers to as a "part of virtue" . . . occupies his attention in the rest of Book V, but it need not concern us here for it is not an aspect of moral virtue

---

[37] See NE, X, 9, 1179ᵇ19–1180ᵃ4.
[38] See NE, I, 3, 1095ᵃ2–11.
[39] NE, II, 3, 1104ᵇ10–11, 15; cf. IV, 1, 1121ᵃ4–5.

except insofar as it is involved in a man's being generally just. "Justice in this sense is not a part of virtue, but virtue entire," yet it is complete virtue "not absolutely, but only in relation to our neighbor."[40]

If, because they are merely distinct aspects of one and the same habit of right desire, a man cannot be temperate without having fortitude, or cannot be courageous without having temperance, then it is also true, for exactly the same reason, that a man cannot be generally just unless he is also temperate and courageous, and he cannot have temperance and fortitude without also being generally just in his dealings with his fellow men and in relation to organized society as a whole. . . . The man who has a good moral character will not only be habitually disposed, in his making of choices, to act as he ought in the pursuit of his own happiness; he will also be habitually disposed to act as he ought in relation to the rights of other men and in relation to the good of the community as a whole—in Aristotle's language, both *fairly* in his transactions with other men, and *lawfully* in relation to the good of the community.[41]

However, that aspect of moral virtue which is justice does not habitually incline a man to act in every way for the good of his fellow men, but only to act in such a way as not to injure them by unfair treatment or the violation of their rights. Only the benevolence of love or perfect friendship impels a man to act positively for the happiness of another, as he would act for his own ultimate good. That is why "when men are friends they have no need of justice, while when they are just they need friendship as well."[42]

—— 6 ——

One further point deserves brief comment, and that is the relation of the two branches of moral philosophy we have come to call

[40] *NE*, V, 1, 1129[b]14–15, 1130[a]10.
[41] See *NE*, V, 2, 1130[b]7–1131[a]9.
[42] *NE*, VIII, 1, 1155[a]25–27.

ethics and politics. Aristotle himself used the term "politics" or "political science" for the branch of learning that is concerned with the ultimate human good, and because it is concerned with the ultimate end, he speaks of it as the "master discipline" or "architectonic science."[43]

Nevertheless, the book in which man's ultimate end and the means to it are given the most extended and detailed treatment is titled *Ethics*, whereas the book in which human happiness is treated only as a measure of the goodness of the state and its constitution is titled *Politics*.

The purely verbal difficulty is resolved if we use the phrase "moral philosophy" to name the one architectonic discipline in the practical order or order of human action, and use "ethics" and "politics" to name related aspects of this one discipline, each of which has a certain primacy, but not in the same respect.

When Aristotle says that "the end is the same for the single man and for the state," he adds that "the end of the state . . . is something greater or more complete, whether to attain or to preserve."[44] Now, if the end is the same for both, and that end is human happiness or the good life, then the only sense in which the end of the state is greater or more complete must reside in the fact that the state aims at the happiness of all its citizens, whereas the single individual aims only at his own or, at most, his own together with the happiness of his immediate friends whose lives are united with his own.

On the other hand, it is not merely for the sake of life, but for the sake of the good life, that the state comes into existence and continues in existence.[45] And it is the good life for individual men (the *totum bonum hominis*), not the good of the community as such (the *bonum communitatis*), which is the ultimate end to be aimed at by all political arrangements.

That is why Aristotle criticizes Plato for maintaining, in the *Republic*, that the ideal state is not concerned with the happiness

---

[43] See *NE*, I, 2.
[44] *NE*, I, 2, 1094^{b}8–9; cf. *Politics*, VII, 2, 1324^{a}5–7.
[45] See *Politics*, I, 2, 1252^{b}20–30; cf. III, 9, 1280^{a}21–32; III, 10, 1280^{b}39–40.

of its guardian class or any other of its component groups. There is no meaning to the happiness of a society as a whole except in terms of the happiness of all, or most, or some of its human members.[46]

Since, then, the ultimate end of the state is the happiness of its individual members, that aspect of moral philosophy (ethics) which deals with the pursuit of happiness *as such* has an obvious primacy, whereas that aspect of moral philosophy (politics) which deals with the external conditions that affect the pursuit of happiness has primacy only in relation to the problem of doing what can be done to make it possible for all men to engage in the pursuit of happiness.

Anyone who is concerned with thinking about the "best form of state," or the ideal conditions men should aim at in their social, economic, and political institutions and arrangements, must first determine "which is the most eligible life," that is, which is the best life for man.[47] When that is determined, as Aristotle has determined it in the *Ethics* (the conclusions of which he summarizes in the *Politics*), the ideal can be simply stated: "That form of government is best in which every man, whoever he is, can act best and live happily."[48]

There is a sense in which the goals of the single individual and of the organized community are not the same. The individual aims at his own happiness and, beyond that, only at the happiness of his friends or loved ones. He does not aim at what Mill called "the general happiness"; that is the objective of the state or organized society, not the individual man. But since moral virtue is the principal operative means in the individual's making a good life for himself, the pursuit of his own happiness and that of his friends involves him also in acting justly toward other members of the community and for the good of the community as a whole.

Thus, it is only in the books concerned with justice and with friendship (V and VIII–IX) that the *Nicomachean Ethics* deals

---

[46] See *Politics*, II, 6, 1264ᵇ16–24.
[47] *Politics*, VII, 1, 1232ᵃ14–22.
[48] Ibid., VII, 2, 1324ᵃ24–25.

with the relation of the individual to other men and to the community, but even when it does so, the focus of attention always centers on the moral virtue or good character of the individual as the factor indispensable to his making a good life for himself.

However, there is another factor indispensable to the individual's making a good life for himself, and that consists of all the things that he needs but does not have the power to obtain wholly for himself, no matter how virtuous he is. These goods, which can all be lumped together as wholly or partly goods of fortune (goods of chance rather than of choice), include such things as freedom from coercion and duress, political liberty, a dignified and basically equal status in the community, equality of educational opportunity, a healthful environment and medical care, a decent share of the available economic goods, as much free time as possible, recreational opportunities, and, last but not least, a state of external and of civil peace.

To provide the conditions under which *all*—all, *not* some—of its human members can succeed in making good lives for themselves, if they also have the moral virtue and moral wisdom requisite for success in that effort, the state, or organized community as a whole, faces a complicated set of practical problems that are quite different from those of the individual man, though both aim at the same ultimate end.

Aristotle's *Politics* not only fails to provide us with satisfactory solutions to most of these social, economic, and political problems; it also advocates views that, if adopted, would prevent their being solved in a manner that would produce the good society—a society in which all men would have an equal opportunity, as far as external conditions were concerned, to engage effectively in the pursuit of happiness. Its chief contribution lies in its one controlling insight that the standard by which a society, in all its aspects, is to be judged as good or bad, better or worse, is the good life for the individual man.

I do not mean to say that the *Politics* does not make a number of important contributions to the theory of the state and of government (such as its account of the origin and nature of the state, and its conceptions of constitutional government, of citizenship, and of political liberty), but it suffers much more from the limitations of the historic circumstances under which it was written than does the *Nicomachean Ethics.* It is relatively easy to universalize the truths to be found in the *Ethics* concerning the good life for man. I would like to think that this book of mine has done that with some measure of success. But to state the truths about the good society in an equally universal manner, one would have to repudiate much that is said in the *Politics*, transform in radical ways the sound conceptions it offers, and deal with many subjects it does not treat at all.

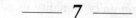

7

In the history of moral philosophy in the West, the *Nicomachean Ethics* has had a checkered career. The soundness of its approach to moral problems and the moral wisdom it offers for their solution were almost totally ignored by the leading schools of thought in the Hellenistic period. The Roman Stoics and Epicureans developed doctrines the flimsiness and fallacies of which would have been apparent to anyone who had read Aristotle's *Ethics* and had discovered its central and controlling insights.

Cicero, who took pride in his effort to translate Greek thought into the Latin language, wrote two moral treatises—*De Officiis* and *De Finibus*—which show little or no evidence of his acquaintance with or understanding of the *Nicomachean Ethics.* In the later Middle Ages, when the works of Aristotle had been recovered and reintroduced into Western thought, Arabic, Jewish, and Christian commentators explicated the text passage by passage, usually erring in the direction of treating it with the same reverence for every sentence that governed their interpretation of Holy Writ.

Nevertheless, in spite of this undue effort to make the text read as if it were a seamless whole from beginning to end, there existed for a brief period a better understanding of the book's pivotal conceptions and guiding principles than can be found in earlier centuries. Yet even this better understanding involved serious changes in emphasis that resulted from subordinating moral philosophy to moral theology in the writings of such devoted followers of Aristotle as Maimonides and Thomas Aquinas. I will return to this point presently.

From the seventeenth century on, the turn is for the worse again, with the *Nicomachean Ethics* either unread or misread by the leading moral philosophers of modern times—by Spinoza in the seventeenth century; by Hume and Kant, in the eighteenth century; by J.S. Mill and Henry Sidgwick, in the nineteenth century; and, in our own century, by John Dewey, G. E. Moore, H. A. Pritchard, and others among contemporary writers on ethics or metaethics.

Failure to refer to Aristotle's *Ethics* where it is plainly relevant to the problems with which these authors are concerned constitutes evidence either of their ignorance of the book or of their lack of sufficient understanding of it to perceive its relevance. Reference to it, accompanied by its dismissal as making little or no contribution to the solution of the problems with which they are concerned shows little or no understanding of its doctrine on their part.

Explicit rejection of it as an erroneous or inadequate approach to moral philosophy, as in the case of Immanuel Kant or John Dewey, is based on their fundamental misapprehensions of Aristotle's theory, which I have taken pains to point out. . . . These misapprehensions not only convert their rejection of Aristotle's *Ethics* into an act of knocking down a straw man, but, in addition, they reappear as fundamental mistakes in their own doctrines—mistakes so crucial that they invalidate those doctrines at their core. I know of only one contemporary work in which the rejection of Aristotle's approach to moral problems is based on a criticism of it that shows an understanding rather than a misunderstanding of his theory, and that is Professor Georg Henrik von Wright's *The Varieties of Goodness.* [4]

I am not saying that Aristotle's *Ethics* is above criticism, that its doctrine as expounded here is without errors or faults, or that it solves all moral problems perfectly. My only claim is that it is sounder in its approach to moral problems, advances more truth in their solution, and does so in a manner that is more practical and less dogmatic than any other ethical treatise in the tradition of Western thought. It is, in short, so substantial a contribution to man's thinking about good and evil, and right and wrong, in the conduct of human life that its shortcomings or faults deserve much better criticism than they have so far received. To be better, the criticism, of course, would have to be based on a better understanding of the *Nicomachean Ethics* than has been manifested in modern times and in contemporary discussion.

I mentioned earlier the changes in emphasis that resulted in the Middle Ages from subordinating moral philosophy to moral theology. Aquinas, for example, heavily stressed what Aristotle had to say about contemplation in Book X of the *Ethics* and, in addition, attached to contemplation a religious significance it could not have had for Aristotle. Furthermore, in view of the Christian dogmas concerning the immortality of the soul and divine rewards and punishments, Aquinas viewed man's terrestrial and temporal happiness, centering either exclusively or primarily in the activity of contemplating God, as nothing but an imperfect and unsatisfactory anticipation of the eternal happiness of heavenly rest in the beatific vision enjoyed by the souls of the blessed in the presence of God.

Looked at one way, this represents a transformation of Aristotle's doctrine, assimilating what truth there is in it to the dogmas of Christian moral theology; but looked at another way, it represents a rejection of Aristotle's position as false in its own terms, since for him the ultimate end—the *totum bonum*—is the temporal whole of a good life on earth, and since, as I have also shown, contemplation for Aristotle is not the contemplation of God but merely knowing for the sake of knowing, which may be the highest form of leisure activity in Aristotle's estimation but which, even so, is only one good among others, each of which is a part of happiness, and all of which contribute to the good life as a whole.

The rejection of the *Nicomachean Ethics* as false in its own terms, because it runs counter to the fundamental dogmas of orthodox, traditional Christianity, can also be based, as it has been by Jacques Maritain in our day, on the grounds that Aristotle proceeds on a hypothesis about human nature that is contrary to fact—the fact in this case being the revealed truth about man. The dogma of original sin and its consequences, which render man dependent on divine grace for even the least measure of success in acting or living well, makes a sound and adequate moral philosophy inherently impossible. [5]

This criticism applies not only to Aristotle's *Ethics*, but to every other attempt on the part of philosophers to deal with the problems of human conduct, good and evil, right and wrong, on the purely secular and natural plane. Whether it is correct or not is hardly an arguable issue, for one side appeals to articles of faith the truth of which the other side does not acknowledge.

Nevertheless, I would offer one reason for seriously questioning the view that a sound and adequate moral philosophy is impossible *as such* (that is, without the transformations and qualifications that a dogmatic moral theology would insist upon). My reason is couched in Aristotelian terms, and it is as follows.

The only standard we have for judging all of our social, economic, and political institutions and arrangements as just or unjust, as good or bad, as better or worse, derives from our conception of the good life for man on earth, and from our conviction that, given certain external conditions, it is possible for men to make good lives for themselves by their own efforts.

It follows that those who take Maritain's view must also maintain that men of diverse religious faiths and men totally devoid of religious faith cannot find a common ground and make common cause against the social, economic, and political injustices that exist all over the world. If they take the opposite view, as Maritain himself does, [6] then there must be sufficient truth in moral philosophy to provide a rational basis for the efforts at social reform and improvement in which all men, regardless of their religious beliefs or disbeliefs, can join. Such common action for a better society presupposes that the measure of a good society consists in the degree to which it promotes the general welfare and serves the happiness of its people—this happiness being their earthly and temporal happiness, for there is no other ultimate end that the secular state can serve. [7]

Endnotes to Appendix II

1. At the Aspen Institute of Humanistic Studies in the summer of 1967, the eminent Confucian scholar Dr. Wing-sit Chan and I conducted a joint seminar devoted to a comparison of the Confucian and Aristotelian conceptions of the good life for man. The major points in the doctrines of

Confucius and of Aristotle were respectively summarized by Dr. Chan and by me, and the members of the seminar were asked to discuss the similarities and differences they noted. It was generally agreed that the outstanding difference between the two philosophers was in their intellectual style and method; on the side of substance, it seemed equally clear to all present that the fundamental notions and insights were either the same or closely parallel.

2. In view of all the conflicting interpretations to which the book has been subject, I certainly cannot claim that mine is the right interpretation of its message. However, I think I can defend the statement that mine is an interpretation that produces a sound and practical moral philosophy, and one that has a great deal of wisdom.

3. *The Letters of William James*, edited by his son Henry James, in two volumes: Vol. II, pp. 352–356.

4. Professor von Wright tells us his reason for turning away from Aristotle's teleological ethics in the direction of Mill's utilitarianism. Having adopted a *teleological* position, he then distinguishes "between two main variants of this position in ethics. The one makes the notion of the good relative to the *nature* of man. The other makes it relative to the needs and wants of individual men. We could call the two variants the 'objectivist' and the 'subjectivist' variant respectively. I think it is right to say that Aristotle favored the first. Here my position differs from his and is, I think, more akin to that of some writers of the utilitarian tradition" (Georg Henrik von Wright, *The Varieties of Goodness*, p. vi).

5. See Jacques Maritain, "Reflections on Moral Philosophy," in *Science and Humanism*, pp. 137–220; and *Moral Philosophy*, Chapters 3, 5.

6. See Jacques Maritain, *Scholasticism and Politics*, pp. 194–248; *Ransoming the Time*, pp. 126–140; *The Range of Reason*, pp. 172–184.

7. The one important text in Aristotle's *Ethics* that has not been mentioned, but not overlooked, in the foregoing commentary is the passage in which Aristotle distinguishes between theoretical (or descriptive) truth and practical (or prescriptive) truth—the truth of propositions in which the word "is" is operative and the truth of propositions in which the word "ought" is operative. He tells us that practical, normative, or prescriptive truth consists in its conformity with right desire; that is, with desiring the real goods we ought to desire, not the merely apparent goods that we may in fact desire (*NE*, VI, 2, 1139^{a}27–31). A correct understanding of this passage leads us to the formulation of the one self-evident categorical imperative that is the only axiomatic principle in Aristotle's *Ethics*; namely, we *ought* to desire that which is really good for us and nothing else.

INDEX

```
                    6946
170    Adler, Mortimer J.
Adl    Desires, right &
       wrong           14.95
```

	DATE DUE	
01 JUL 1993		